Practice the

California High School Exit Exam Practice Test Questions

Published by

Copyright Notice

Copyright © 2013, by *Blue Butterfly Books*™, Sheila M. Hynes. ALL RIGHTS RESERVED. No part of this book may be reproduced or transferred in any form or by any means, graphic, electronic, or mechanical, including photocopying, recording, web distribution, taping, or by any information storage retrieval system, without the written permission of the author.

Notice: *Blue Butterfly Books*™ makes every reasonable effort to obtain from reliable sources accurate, complete, and timely information about the tests covered in this book. Nevertheless, changes can be made in the tests or the administration of the tests at any time and *Blue Butterfly Books*™ makes no representation or warranty, either expressed or implied as to the accuracy, timeliness, or completeness of the information contained in this book. *Blue Butterfly Books*™ makes no representations or warranties of any kind, express or implied, about the completeness, accuracy, reliability, suitability or availability with respect to the information contained in this document for any purpose. Any reliance you place on such information is therefore strictly at your own risk.

The author(s) shall not be liable for any loss incurred as a consequence of the use and application, directly or indirectly, of any information presented in this work. Sold with the understanding, the author is not engaged in rendering professional services or advice. If advice or expert assistance is required, the services of a competent professional should be sought.

The company, product and service names used in this book are for identification purposes only. All trademarks and registered trademarks are the property of their respective owners. *Blue Butterfly Books*™ is not affiliate with any educational institution.

We strongly recommend that students check with exam providers for up-to-date information regarding test content.

ISBN-13: 978-1490344799
ISBN-10: 1490344799

Published by

Blue Butterfly Books
Victoria BC Canada

Visit us on the web at http://www.test-preparation.ca
Printed in the USA

Version 6.0 October 2014

The CAHSEE Exam is administered by the California Department of Education, who are not involved in the production of, and do not endorse this publication.

Sustainability and Eco-Responsibility

Here at *Blue Butterfly Books*™, trees are valuable to Mother Earth and the health and wellbeing of everyone. Minimizing our ecological footprint and effect on the environment, we choose *CreateSpace*, an eco-responsible printing company.

Electronic routing of our books reduces greenhouse gas emissions, worldwide. When a book order is received, the order is filled at the printing location closest to the client. *Blue Butterfly Books*™ are printed as they are requested, saving thousands of books, and trees over time. This process offers a stable and viable alternative, keeping healthy sustainability of our environment.

Find us on Facebook

Go to http://tinyurl.com/cadyjlj

Contents

7   **Getting Started**
        The CAHSEE® Study Plan   8
        Making a Study Schedule   10

14   **Practice Test Questions Set 1**
        Answer Key   62

79   **Practice Test Questions Set 2**
        Answer Key   125

144   **Conclusion**

Getting Started

CONGRATULATIONS! By deciding to take the California High School Exit Exam (CAHSEE®), you have taken the first step toward a great future! Of course, there is no point in taking this important examination unless you intend to do your very best to earn the highest grade you possibly can. That means getting yourself organized and discovering the best approaches, methods and strategies to master the material. Yes, that will require real effort and dedication on your part but if you are willing to focus your energy and devote the study time necessary, before you know it you will be on you way to a brighter future!

We know that taking on a new endeavour can be a little scary, and it is easy to feel unsure of where to begin. That's where we come in. This study guide is designed to help you improve your test-taking skills, show you a few tricks of the trade and increase both your competency and confidence.

The California High School Exit Exam

The CAHSEE® exam is composed of three modules, reading, mathematics and writing. The reading section consists of reading comprehension questions. The mathematics section contains basic math, algebra, geometry and problem solving. The writing section contains an essay question, English grammar and usage multiple choice, and essay revision questions.

While we seek to make our guide as comprehensive as possible, it is important to note that like all entrance exams, the CAHSEE® Exam might be adjusted at some future point. New material might be added, or content that is no longer relevant or applicable might be removed. It is always a good idea to give the materials you receive when you register to take the CAHSEE® a careful review.

The CAHSEE® Study Plan

Now that you have made the decision to take the CAHSEE®, it is time to get started. Before you do another thing, you will need to figure out a plan of attack. The very best study tip is to start early! The longer the time period you devote to regular study practice, the more likely you will be to retain the material and be able to access it quickly. If you thought that 1x20 is the same as 2x10, guess what? It really is not, when it comes to study time. Reviewing material for just an hour per day over the course of 20 days is far better than studying for two hours a day for only 10 days. The more often you revisit a particular piece of information, the better you will know it. Not only will your grasp and understanding be better, but your ability to reach into your brain and quickly and efficiently pull out the tidbit you need, will be greatly enhanced as well.

The great Chinese scholar and philosopher Confucius believed that true knowledge could be defined as knowing both what you know and what you do not know. The first step in preparing for the CAHSEE® is to assess your strengths and weaknesses. You may already have an idea of what you know and what you do not know, but evaluating yourself using our Self- Assessment modules for each of the three areas, Math, Writing and Reading Comprehension, will clarify the details.

Making a Study Schedule

To make your study time most productive you will need to develop a study plan. The purpose of the plan is to organize all the bits of pieces of information in such a way that you will not feel overwhelmed. Rome was not built in a day, and learning everything you will need to know to pass the CAHSEE® is going to take time, too. Arranging the material you need to learn into manageable chunks is the best way to go. Each study session should make you feel as though you have succeeded in accomplishing your goal, and your goal is simply to learn what you planned to learn during that particular session. Try to organize the content in such a way that each study session builds upon previous ones. That way, you will retain the information, be better able to access it, and review the previous bits and pieces at the same time.

Self-assessment

The Best Study Tip! The very best study tip is to start early! The longer you study regularly, the more you will retain and 'learn' the material. Studying for 1 hour per day for 20 days is far better than studying for 2 hours for 10 days.

What don't you know?

The first step is to assess your strengths and weaknesses. You may already have an idea of where your weaknesses are, or you can take our Self-assessment modules for each of the areas, Math, English, Science and Reading Comprehension.

Exam Component	Rate from 1 to 5
Reading Comprehension	
Vocabulary (Meaning in Context)	
Main idea	
Mathematics	
Decimals Percent and Fractions	
Interpreting Graphs and Tables	
Mean, mode and median	

Basic Algebra	
Geometry	
Problem Solving	
Writing Essay writing	
Sentence structure & usage	

Making a Study Schedule

The key to making a study plan is to divide the material you need to learn into manageable size and learn it, while at the same time reviewing the material that you already know.

Using the table above, any scores of three or below, you need to spend time learning, going over and practicing this subject area. A score of four means you need to review the material, but you don't have to spend time re-learning. A score of five and you are OK with just an occasional review before the exam.

A score of zero or one means you really do need to work on this and you should allocate the most time and give it the highest priority. Some students prefer a 5-day plan and others a 10-day plan. It also depends on how much time you have until the exam.

Here is an example of a 5-day plan based on an example from the table above:

Main Idea: 1   Study 1 hour everyday – review on last day
Fractions: 3   Study 1 hour for 2 days then ½ hour and then review
Algebra: 4   Review every second day
Grammar & Usage: 2 Study 1 hour on the first day – then ½ hour everyday

Reading Comprehension: 5   Review for ½ hour every other day
Geometry: 5 Review for ½ hour every other day

Using this example, geometry and reading comprehension are good and only need occasional review. Algebra is good and needs 'some' review. Fractions need a bit of work, grammar and usage needs a lot of work and Main Idea is very weak and need the most time. Based on this, here is a sample study plan:

Day	Subject	Time
Monday		
Study	Main Idea	1 hour
Study	Grammar & Usage	1 hour
	½ hour break	
Study	Fractions	1 hour
Review	Algebra	½ hour
Tuesday		
Study	Main Idea	1 hour
Study	Grammar & Usage	½ hour
	½ hour break	
Study	Fractions	½ hour
Review	Algebra	½ hour
Review	Geometry	½ hour
Wednesday		
Study	Main Idea	1 hour
Study	Grammar & Usage	½ hour
	½ hour break	
Study	Fractions	½ hour
Review	Geometry	½ hour
Thursday		
Study	Main Idea	½ hour
Study	Grammar & Usage	½ hour
Review	Fractions	½ hour
	½ hour break	
Review	Geometry	½ hour

Review	Algebra	½ hour
Friday		
Review	Main Idea	½ hour
Review	Grammar & Usage	½ hour
Review	Fractions	½ hour
	½ hour break	
Review	Algebra	½ hour
Review	Grammar & Usage	½ hour

Using this example, adapt the study plan to your own schedule. This schedule assumes 2 ½ - 3 hours available to study everyday for a 5 day period.

First, write out what you need to study and how much. Next figure out how many days you have before the test. Note, do NOT study on the last day before the test. On the last day before the test, you won't learn anything and will probably only confuse yourself.

Make a table with the days before the test and the number of hours you have available to study each day. We suggest working with 1 hour and ½ hour time slots.

Start filling in the blanks, with the subjects you need to study the most getting the most time and the most regular time slots (i.e. everyday) and the subjects that you know getting the least time (e.g. ½ hour every other day, or every 3rd day).

Tips for making a schedule

Once you make a schedule, stick with it! Make your study sessions reasonable. If you make a study schedule and don't stick with it, you set yourself up for failure. Instead, schedule study sessions that are a bit shorter and set yourself up for success! Make sure your study sessions are do-able. Studying is hard work but after you pass, you can party and take a break!

Schedule breaks. Breaks are just as important as study time. Work out a rotation of studying and breaks that works for you.

Build up study time. If you find it hard to sit still and study for 1 hour straight through, build up to it. Start with 20 minutes, and then take a break. Once you get used to 20-minute study sessions, increase the time to 30 minutes. Gradually work you way up to 1 hour.

40 minutes to 1 hour are optimal. Studying for longer than this is tiring and not productive. Studying for shorter isn't long enough to be productive.

Studying Math. Studying Math is different from studying other subjects because you use a different part of your brain. The best way to study math is to practice everyday. This will train your mind to think in a mathematical way. If you miss a day or days, the mathematical mind-set is gone and you have to start all over again to build it up.

Study and practice math everyday for at least 5 days before the exam.

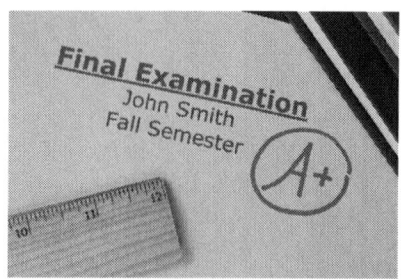

Practice Test Questions Set 1

The questions below are not the same as you will find on the CAHSEE® - that would be too easy! And nobody knows what the questions will be and they change all the time. Below are general questions that cover the same subject areas as the CAHSEE®. So, while the format and exact wording of the questions may differ slightly, and change from year to year, if you can answer the questions below, you will have no problem with the CAHSEE®.

For the best results, take these Practice Test Questions as if it were the real exam. Set aside time when you will not be disturbed, and a location that is quiet and free of distractions. Read the instructions carefully, read each question carefully, and answer to the best of your ability.
Use the bubble answer sheets provided. When you have completed the Practice Questions, check your answer against the Answer Key and read the explanation provided.

Do not attempt more than one set of practice test questions in one day. After completing the first practice test, wait two or three days before attempting the second set of questions.

Reading Answer Sheet

1. Ⓐ Ⓑ Ⓒ Ⓓ   11. Ⓐ Ⓑ Ⓒ Ⓓ   21. Ⓐ Ⓑ Ⓒ Ⓓ
2. Ⓐ Ⓑ Ⓒ Ⓓ   12. Ⓐ Ⓑ Ⓒ Ⓓ   22. Ⓐ Ⓑ Ⓒ Ⓓ
3. Ⓐ Ⓑ Ⓒ Ⓓ   13. Ⓐ Ⓑ Ⓒ Ⓓ   23. Ⓐ Ⓑ Ⓒ Ⓓ
4. Ⓐ Ⓑ Ⓒ Ⓓ   14. Ⓐ Ⓑ Ⓒ Ⓓ   24. Ⓐ Ⓑ Ⓒ Ⓓ
5. Ⓐ Ⓑ Ⓒ Ⓓ   15. Ⓐ Ⓑ Ⓒ Ⓓ   25. Ⓐ Ⓑ Ⓒ Ⓓ
6. Ⓐ Ⓑ Ⓒ Ⓓ   16. Ⓐ Ⓑ Ⓒ Ⓓ   26. Ⓐ Ⓑ Ⓒ Ⓓ
7. Ⓐ Ⓑ Ⓒ Ⓓ   17. Ⓐ Ⓑ Ⓒ Ⓓ   27. Ⓐ Ⓑ Ⓒ Ⓓ
8. Ⓐ Ⓑ Ⓒ Ⓓ   18. Ⓐ Ⓑ Ⓒ Ⓓ   28. Ⓐ Ⓑ Ⓒ Ⓓ
9. Ⓐ Ⓑ Ⓒ Ⓓ   19. Ⓐ Ⓑ Ⓒ Ⓓ   29. Ⓐ Ⓑ Ⓒ Ⓓ
10. Ⓐ Ⓑ Ⓒ Ⓓ   20. Ⓐ Ⓑ Ⓒ Ⓓ   30. Ⓐ Ⓑ Ⓒ Ⓓ

Mathematics Answer Sheet

1. A B C D
2. A B C D
3. A B C D
4. A B C D
5. A B C D
6. A B C D
7. A B C D
8. A B C D
9. A B C D
10. A B C D
11. A B C D
12. A B C D
13. A B C D
14. A B C D
15. A B C D
16. A B C D
17. A B C D

18. A B C D
19. A B C D
20. A B C D
21. A B C D
22. A B C D
23. A B C D
24. A B C D
25. A B C D
26. A B C D
27. A B C D
28. A B C D
29. A B C D
30. A B C D
31. A B C D
32. A B C D
33. A B C D
34. A B C D

35. A B C D
36. A B C D
37. A B C D
38. A B C D
39. A B C D
40. A B C D
41. A B C D
42. A B C D
43. A B C D
44. A B C D
45. A B C D
46. A B C D
47. A B C D
48. A B C D
49. A B C D
50. A B C D

Essay Revision - English Grammar and Usage Answer Sheet

1. Ⓐ Ⓑ Ⓒ Ⓓ   11. Ⓐ Ⓑ Ⓒ Ⓓ   21. Ⓐ Ⓑ Ⓒ Ⓓ
2. Ⓐ Ⓑ Ⓒ Ⓓ   12. Ⓐ Ⓑ Ⓒ Ⓓ   22. Ⓐ Ⓑ Ⓒ Ⓓ
3. Ⓐ Ⓑ Ⓒ Ⓓ   13. Ⓐ Ⓑ Ⓒ Ⓓ   23. Ⓐ Ⓑ Ⓒ Ⓓ
4. Ⓐ Ⓑ Ⓒ Ⓓ   14. Ⓐ Ⓑ Ⓒ Ⓓ   24. Ⓐ Ⓑ Ⓒ Ⓓ
5. Ⓐ Ⓑ Ⓒ Ⓓ   15. Ⓐ Ⓑ Ⓒ Ⓓ   25. Ⓐ Ⓑ Ⓒ Ⓓ
6. Ⓐ Ⓑ Ⓒ Ⓓ   16. Ⓐ Ⓑ Ⓒ Ⓓ   26. Ⓐ Ⓑ Ⓒ Ⓓ
7. Ⓐ Ⓑ Ⓒ Ⓓ   17. Ⓐ Ⓑ Ⓒ Ⓓ   27. Ⓐ Ⓑ Ⓒ Ⓓ
8. Ⓐ Ⓑ Ⓒ Ⓓ   18. Ⓐ Ⓑ Ⓒ Ⓓ   28. Ⓐ Ⓑ Ⓒ Ⓓ
9. Ⓐ Ⓑ Ⓒ Ⓓ   19. Ⓐ Ⓑ Ⓒ Ⓓ   29. Ⓐ Ⓑ Ⓒ Ⓓ
10. Ⓐ Ⓑ Ⓒ Ⓓ   20. Ⓐ Ⓑ Ⓒ Ⓓ   30. Ⓐ Ⓑ Ⓒ Ⓓ

Part 1 - Reading

Questions 1 – 4 refer to the following passage.

Infectious Diseases

An infectious disease is a clinically evident illness resulting from the presence of pathogenic agents, such as viruses, bacteria, fungi, protozoa, multi-cellular parasites, and unusual proteins known as prions. Infectious pathologies are also called communicable diseases or transmissible diseases, due to their potential of transmission from one person or species to another by a replicating agent (as opposed to a toxin).

Transmission of an infectious disease can occur in many different ways. Physical contact, liquids, food, body fluids, contaminated objects, and airborne inhalation can all transmit infecting agents.

Transmissible diseases that occur through contact with an ill person, or objects touched by them, are especially infective, and are sometimes called contagious diseases. Communicable diseases that require a more specialized route of infection, such as through blood or needle transmission, or sexual transmission, are usually not regarded as contagious.

The term infectivity describes the ability of an organism to enter, survive and multiply in the host, while the infectiousness of a disease indicates the comparative ease with which the disease is transmitted. An infection however, is not synonymous with an infectious disease, as an infection may not cause important clinical symptoms. [1]

Practice Test Questions 1   19

1. What can we infer from the first paragraph in this passage?

    a. Sickness from a toxin can be easily transmitted from one person to another.

    b. Sickness from an infectious disease can be easily transmitted from one person to another.

    c. Few sicknesses are transmitted from one person to another.

    d. Infectious diseases are easily treated.

2. What are two other names for infections' pathologies?

    a. Communicable diseases or transmissible diseases

    b. Communicable diseases or terminal diseases

    c. Transmissible diseases or preventable diseases

    d. Communicative diseases or unstable diseases

3. What does infectivity describe?

    a. The inability of an organism to multiply in the host

    b. The inability of an organism to reproduce

    c. The ability of an organism to enter, survive and multiply in the host

    d. The ability of an organism to reproduce in the host

4. How do we know an infection is not synonymous with an infectious disease?

    a. Because an infectious disease destroys infections with enough time.

    b. Because an infection may not cause clinical symptoms or impair host function.

    c. We do not. The two are synonymous.

    d. Because an infection is too fatal to be an infectious disease.

Questions 5 – 7 refer to the following passage.

Thunderstorms

The first stage of a thunderstorm is the cumulus stage, or developing stage. In this stage, masses of moisture are lifted upwards into the atmosphere. The trigger for this lift can be insulation heating the ground producing thermals, areas where two winds converge, forcing air upwards, or where winds blow over terrain of increasing elevation. Moisture in the air rapidly cools into liquid drops of water, which appears as cumulus clouds.

As the water vapor condenses into liquid, latent heat is released which warms the air, causing it to become less dense than the surrounding dry air. The warm air rises in an updraft through the process of convection (hence the term convective precipitation). This creates a low-pressure zone beneath the forming thunderstorm. In a typical thunderstorm, approximately 5×10^8 kg of water vapor is lifted, and the amount of energy released when this condenses is about equal to the energy used by a city of 100,000 in a month. [2]

5. The cumulus stage of a thunderstorm is the

    a. The last stage of the storm

    b. The middle stage of the storm formation

    c. The beginning of the thunderstorm

    d. The period after the thunderstorm has ended

6. One of the ways the air is warmed is

    a. Air moving downwards, which creates a high-pressure zone

    b. Air cooling and becoming less dense, causing it to rise

    c. Moisture moving downward toward the earth

    d. Heat created by water vapor condensing into liquid

7. Identify the correct sequence of events.

a. Warm air rises, water droplets condense, creating more heat, and the air rises further.

b. Warm air rises and cools, water droplets condense, causing low pressure.

c. Warm air rises and collects water vapor, the water vapor condenses as the air rises, which creates heat, and causes the air to rise further.

d. None of the above.

Questions 8 – 10 refer to the following passage.

The US Weather Service

The United States National Weather Service classifies thunderstorms as severe when they reach a predetermined level. Usually, this means the storm is strong enough to inflict wind or hail damage. In most of the United States, a storm is considered severe if winds reach over 50 knots (58 mph or 93 km/h), hail is ¾ inch (2 cm) diameter or larger, or if meteorologists report funnel clouds or tornadoes. In the Central Region of the United States National Weather Service, the hail threshold for a severe thunderstorm is 1 inch (2.5 cm) in diameter. Though a funnel cloud or tornado indicates the presence of a severe thunderstorm, the various meteorological agencies would issue a tornado warning rather than a severe thunderstorm warning here.

Meteorologists in Canada define a severe thunderstorm as either having tornadoes, wind gusts of 90 km/h or greater, hail 2 centimeters in diameter or greater, rainfall more than 50 millimeters in 1 hour, or 75 millimeters in 3 hours.

Severe thunderstorms can develop from any type of thunderstorm. [3]

8. What is the purpose of this passage?

    a. Explaining when a thunderstorm turns into a tornado

    b. Explaining who issues storm warnings, and when these warnings should be issued

    c. Explaining when meteorologists consider a thunderstorm severe

    d. None of the above

9. It is possible to infer from this passage that

    a. Different areas and countries have different criteria for determining a severe storm

    b. Thunderstorms can include lightning and tornadoes, as well as violent winds and large hail

    c. If someone spots both a thunderstorm and a tornado, meteorological agencies will immediately issue a severe storm warning

    d. Canada has a much different alert system for severe storms, with criteria that are far less

10. What would the Central Region of the United States National Weather Service do if hail was 2.7 cm in diameter?

    a. Not issue a severe thunderstorm warning.

    b. Issue a tornado warning.

    c. Issue a severe thunderstorm warning.

    d. Sleet must also accompany the hail before the Weather Service will issue a storm warning.

Contents

    Science Self-assessment 81
    Answer Key 91
    Science Tutorials 96
    Scientific Method 96
    Biology 99
    Heredity: Genes and Mutation 104
    Classification 108
    Ecology 110
    Chemistry 112
    Energy: Kinetic and Mechanical 126
    Energy: Work and Power 130
    Force: Newton's Three Laws 132

11. Consider the table of contents above. What page would you find information about natural selection and adaptation?

    a. 81
    b. 90
    c. 110
    d. 132

Questions 12 – 14 refer to the following passage.

Clouds

A cloud is a visible mass of droplets or frozen crystals floating in the atmosphere above the surface of the Earth or other planetary bodies. Another type of cloud is a mass of material in space, attracted by gravity, called interstellar clouds and nebulae. The branch of meteorology which studies clouds is called nephrology. When we are speaking of Earth clouds, water vapor is usually the condensing substance, which forms small droplets or ice crystal. These crystals are typically 0.01 mm in diameter. Dense, deep clouds reflect most light, so they appear white, at least from the top. Cloud droplets scatter light very efficiently, so the further into a cloud light travels, the weaker it gets. This accounts for the gray or dark appearance at the base of large clouds. Thin clouds may appear to have acquired the color of their environment or background. [4]

12. What are clouds made of?

    a. Water droplets.

    b. Ice crystals.

    c. Ice crystals and water droplets.

    d. Clouds on Earth are made of ice crystals and water droplets.

13. The main idea of this passage is

    a. Condensation occurs in clouds, having an intense effect on the weather on the surface of the earth.

    b. Atmospheric gases are responsible for the gray color of clouds just before a severe storm happens.

    c. A cloud is a visible mass of droplets or frozen crystals floating in the atmosphere above the surface of the Earth or other planetary body.

    d. Clouds reflect light in varying amounts and degrees, depending on the size and concentration of the water droplets.

14. Why are clouds white on top and grey on the bottom?

    a. Because water droplets inside the cloud do not reflect light, it appears white, and the farther into the cloud the light travels, the less light is reflected making the bottom appear dark.

    b. Because water droplets outside the cloud reflect light, it appears dark, and the farther into the cloud the light travels, the more light is reflected making the bottom appear white.

    c. Because water droplets inside the cloud reflects light, making it appear white, and the farther into the cloud the light travels, the more light is reflected making the bottom appear dark.

d. None of the above.

Questions 15 - 18 refer to the following recipe.

Chocolate Chip Cookies

3/4 cup sugar
3/4 cup packed brown sugar
1 cup butter, softened
2 large eggs, beaten
1 teaspoon vanilla extract
2 1/4 cups all-purpose flour
1 teaspoon baking soda
3/4 teaspoon salt
2 cups semisweet chocolate chips
If desired, 1 cup chopped pecans, or chopped walnuts.
Preheat oven to 375 degrees.

Mix sugar, brown sugar, butter, vanilla and eggs in a large bowl. Stir in flour, baking soda, and salt. The dough will be very stiff.

Stir in chocolate chips by hand with a sturdy wooden spoon. Add the pecans, or other nuts, if desired. Stir until the chocolate chips and nuts are evenly dispersed.

Drop dough by rounded tablespoonfuls 2 inches apart onto a cookie sheet.

Bake 8 to 10 minutes or until light brown. Cookies may look underdone, but they will finish cooking after you take them out of the oven.

15. What is the correct order for adding these ingredients?

    a. Brown sugar, baking soda, chocolate chips
    b. Baking soda, brown sugar, chocolate chips
    c. Chocolate chips, baking soda, brown sugar
    d. Baking soda, chocolate chips, brown sugar

16. What does sturdy mean?

    a. Long
    b. Strong
    c. Short
    d. Wide

17. What does disperse mean?

    a. Scatter
    b. To form a ball
    c. To stir
    d. To beat

18. When can you stop stirring the nuts?

    a. When the cookies are cooked.
    b. When the nuts are evenly distributed.
    c. As soon as the nuts are added.
    d. After the chocolate chips are added.

Questions 19 – 20 refer to the following email.

SUBJECT: MEDICAL STAFF CHANGES

To all staff:

This email is to advise you of a paper on recommended medical staff changes has been posted to the Human Resources website.

The contents are of primary interest to medical staff, other staff may be interested in reading it, particularly those in medical support roles.

The paper deals with several major issues:

1. Improving our ability to attract top quality staff to the hospital, and retain our existing staff. These changes will make our position and departmental names internationally recognizable and comparable with North American and North Asian departments and positions.

2. Improving our ability to attract top quality staff by introducing greater flexibility in the departmental structure.

3. General comments on issues to be further discussed in relation to research staff.

The changes outlined in this paper are significant. I encourage you to read the document and send to me any comments you may have, so that it can be enhanced and improved.

Gordon Simms
Administrator,
Seven Oaks Regional Hospital

19. Are all hospital staff required to read the document posted to the Human Resources website?

  a. Yes all staff are required to read the document.
  b. No, reading the document is optional.
  c. Only medical staff are required to read the document.
  d. none of the above are correct.

20. Have the changes to medical staff been made?

   a. Yes, the changes have been made.

   b. No, the changes are only being discussed.

   c. Some of the changes have been made.

   d. None of the choices are correct.

Questions 21 – 25 refer to the following passage.

Navy Seals

The United States Navy's Sea, Air and Land Teams, commonly known as Navy SEALs, are the U.S. Navy's principal special operations force, and a part of the Naval Special Warfare Command (NSWC) as well as the maritime component of the United States Special Operations Command (USSOCOM).

The unit's acronym ("SEAL") comes from their capacity to operate at sea, in the air, and on land – but it is their ability to work underwater that separates SEALs from most other military units in the world. Navy SEALs are trained and have been deployed in a wide variety of missions, including direct action and special reconnaissance operations, unconventional warfare, foreign internal defence, hostage rescue, counter-terrorism and other missions. All SEALs are members of either the United States Navy or the United States Coast Guard.

In the early morning of May 2, 2011 local time, a team of 40 CIA-led Navy SEALs completed an operation to kill Osama bin Laden in Abbottabad, Pakistan about 35 miles (56 km) from Islamabad, the country's capital. The Navy SEALs were part of the Naval Special Warfare Development Group, previously called "Team 6". President Barack Obama later confirmed the death of bin Laden. The unprecedented media coverage raised the public profile of the SEAL community, particularly the counter-terrorism specialists commonly known as SEAL Team 6. [5]

21. Are Navy SEALs part of USSOCOM?

   a. Yes
   b. No
   c. Only for special operations
   d. No, they are part of the US Navy

22. What separates Navy SEALs from other military units?

   a. Belonging to NSWC
   b. Direct action and special reconnaissance operations
   c. Working underwater
   d. Working for other military units in the world

23. What other military organizations do SEALs belong to?

   a. The US Navy
   b. The Coast Guard
   c. The US Army
   d. The Navy and the Coast Guard

24. What other organization participated in the Bin Laden raid?

   a. The CIA
   b. The US Military
   c. Counter-terrorism specialists
   d. None of the above

25. What is the new name for Team 6?

   a. They were always called Team 6
   b. The counter-terrorism specialists
   c. The Naval Special Warfare Development Group
   d. None of the above

Questions 26 – 28 refer to the following passage.

How To Get A Good Nights Sleep

Sleep is just as essential for healthy living as water, air and food. Sleep allows the body to rest and replenish depleted energy levels. Sometimes we may for various reasons experience difficulty sleeping which has a serious effect on our health. Those who have prolonged sleeping problems are facing a serious medical condition and should see a qualified doctor as soon as possible for help. Here is simple guide that can help you sleep better at night.

Try to create a natural pattern of waking up and sleeping around the same time everyday. This means avoiding going to bed too early and oversleeping past your usual wake up time. Going to bed and getting up at radically different times everyday confuses your body clock. Try to establish a natural rhythm as much as you can.

Exercises and a bit of physical activity can help you sleep better at night. If you are having problem sleeping, try to be as active as you can during the day. If you are tired from physical activity, falling asleep is a natural and easy process for your body. If you remain inactive during the day, you will find it harder to sleep properly at night. Try walking, jogging, swimming or simple stretches as you get close to your bed time.

Afternoon naps are great to refresh you during the day, but they may also keep you awake at night. If you feel sleepy during the day, get up, take a walk and get busy to keep from sleeping. Stretching is a good way to increase blood flow to the brain and keep you alert so that you don't sleep during the day. This will help you sleep better night.

A warm bath or a glass of milk in the evening can help your body relax and prepare for sleep. A cold bath will wake you up and keep you up for several hours. Also avoid eating too late before bed.

26. How would you describe this sentence?

    a. A recommendation

    b. An opinion

    c. A fact

    d. A diagnosis

27. Which of the following is an alternative title for this article?

    a. Exercise and a good night's sleep

    b. Benefits of a good night's sleep

    c. Tips for a good night's sleep

    d. Lack of sleep is a serious medical condition

28. Which of the following can not be inferred from this article?

    a. Biking is helpful for getting a good night's sleep

    b. Mental activity is helpful for getting a good night's sleep

    c. Eating bedtime snacks is not recommended

    d. Getting up at the same time is helpful for a good night's sleep

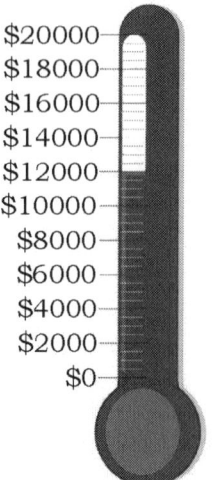

29. Consider the graphic above. The Save the Children fund has a fund-raising goal of $20,000. Approximately how much of their goal have they achieved?

    a. 3/5
    b. 3/4
    c. 1/2
    d. 1/3

30. Consider the graphic above. The Save the Children fund has a fund-raising goal of $16,000. Approximately how much of their goal have they achieved?

    a. 3/5
    b. 3/4
    c. 1/2
    d. 1/3

Mathematics

1. 9,177 + 7,204 =

    a. 16,4712
    b. 16,371
    c. 16,381
    d. 15,412

2. Brad has agreed to buy everyone a Coke. Each drink costs $1.89, and there are 5 friends. Estimate Brad's cost.

    a. $7
    b. $8
    c. $10
    d. $12

3. 643 - 587 =

    a. 56
    b. 66
    c. 46
    d. 55

4. Divide 243 by 3^3

    a. 243
    b. 11
    c. 9
    d. 27

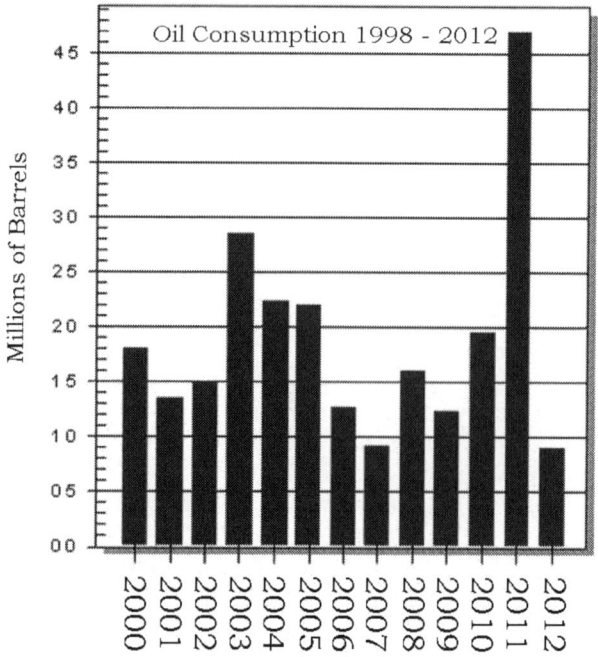

5. The graph above shows oil consumption in millions of barrels for the period, 1998 - 2012. What year did oil consumption peak?

    a. 2011
    b. 2010
    c. 2008
    d. 2009

6. Sarah weighs 25 pounds more than Tony does. If together they weigh 205 pounds, how much does Sarah weigh approximately in kilograms? Assume 1 pound = 0.4535 kilograms.

    a. 41
    b. 48
    c. 50
    d. 52

7. Choose the expression the figure represents.

    a. X ≤ 1
    b. X < 1
    c. X > 1
    d. X ≥ 1

8. Calculate (14 + 2) x 2 + 3

    a. 21
    b. 35
    c. 80
    d. 43

9. What fraction of $1500 is $75?

    a. 1/14
    b. 3/5
    c. 7/10
    d. 1/20

10. Find x and y in the following system of equations:

2x + 3 = y + 6
-4x - 12 = -8y

    a. (3,2)
    b. (1,3)
    c. (3,3)
    d. (2,2)

11. 491 ÷ 9 =

    a. 54 r5
    b. 56 r6
    c. 57 r5
    d. 51 r3

12. Below is the attendance for a class of 45.

Day	Number of Absent Students
Monday	5
Tuesday	9
Wednesday	4
Thursday	10
Friday	6

What is the average attendance for the week?

    a. 88%
    b. 85%
    c. 81%
    d. 77%

13. John purchased a jacket at a 7% discount. He had a membership which gave him an additional 2% discount on the discounted price. If he paid $425, what is the retail price of the jacket?

    a. $460
    b. $466
    c. $466
    d. $472

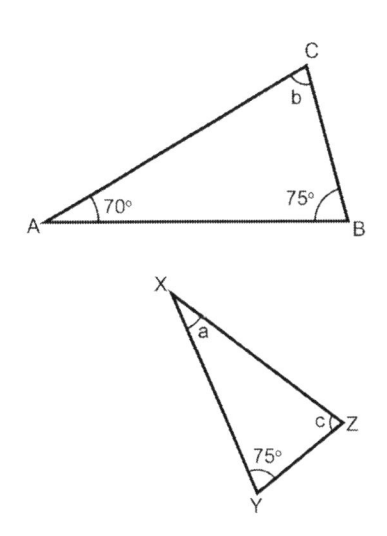

14. What are the respective values of a, b & c if both triangles are similar?

    a. 70°, 70°, 35°
    b. 70°, 35°, 70°
    c. 35°, 35°, 35°
    d. 70°, 35°, 35°

15. $7^5 - 3^5 =$

    a. 15,000
    b. 15,807
    c. 15,800
    d. 15,007

```
        C
       /\
      /  \
     /    \ 9 cm
    /      \
   /        \
  /_____\
 A            B
```

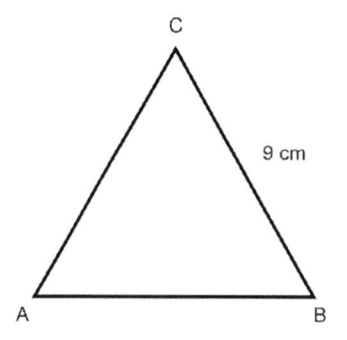

16. What is the perimeter of the equilateral △ABC above?

   a. 18 cm
   b. 12 cm
   c. 27 cm
   d. 15 cm

17. Consider 2 triangles, ABC and A'B'C', where:

   BC = B' C'
   AC = A' C'
   RA = RA'

Are these 2 triangles congruent?

   a. Yes
   b. No
   c. Not enough information

18. Convert from scientific notation: 5.63 x 10⁶

   a. 5,630,000
   b. 563,000
   c. 5630
   d. 0.000005.630

19. Solve the following equation 4(y + 6) = 3y + 30

   a. y = 20
   b. y = 6
   c. y = 30/7
   d. y = 30

20. 10 x 2 − (7 + 9)

   a. 21
   b. 16
   c. 4
   d. 13

21. A map uses a scale of 1:2,000 How much distance on the ground is 5.2 inches on the map if the scale is in inches?

   a. 100,400
   b. 10, 500
   c. 10,440
   d. 1,400

6 cm   C

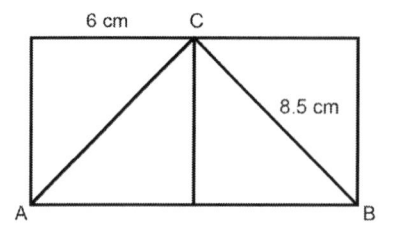

8.5 cm

A   B

22. What is perimeter of △ABC in the above shape?

    a. 25.5 cm
    b. 27 cm
    c. 30 cm
    d. 29 cm

23. Solve for x if, $10^2 \times 100^2 = 1000^x$

    a. x = 2
    b. x = 3
    c. x = -2
    d. x = 0

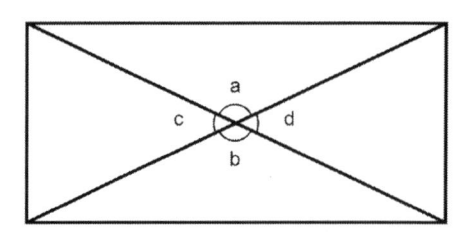

a
c   d
b

24. What is the sum of angles a, b, c and d in the rectangle above?

    a. 180°
    b. 360°
    c. 90°
    d. 120°

25. Express 5 x 5 x 5 x 5 x 5 x 5 in exponential form.

   a. 5^6
   b. 10^6
   c. 5^{16}
   d. 5^3

26. 1278 + 4920 =

   a. 6298
   b. 6108
   c. 6198
   d. 6098

27. A shop sells an equipment for $545. If 15% of the cost was added to the price as value added tax, what is the actual cost of the equipment?

   a. $490.4
   b. $473.9
   c. $505
   d. $503.15

28. Express 9 x 9 x 9 in exponential form and standard form.

   a. $9^3 = 719$
   b. $9^3 = 629$
   c. $9^3 = 729$
   d. $10^3 = 729$

29. 5 men have to share a load weighing 10 kg 550 g equally among themselves. How much weight will each man have to carry?

    a. 900 g
    b. 1.5 kg
    c. 3 kg
    d. 2 kg 110 g

30. Divide 0.524 by 10^3

    a. 0.0524
    b. 0.00052
    c. 0.00524
    d. 524

31. Find the solution for the following linear equation: 5x/2 = 3x + 24/6

    a. -1
    b. 0
    c. 1
    d. 2

32. $3^2 \times 3^5$

    a. 3^{17}
    b. 3^5
    c. 4^8
    d. 3^7

25 cm

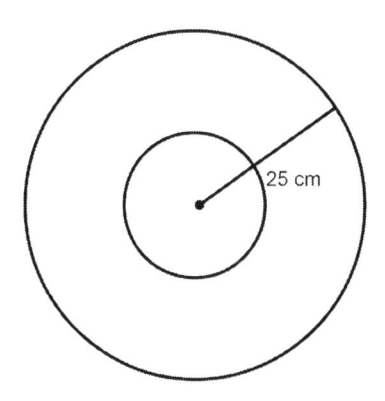

33. What is the distance travelled by the wheel above, when it makes 175 revolutions?

    a. 87.5 π m
    b. 875 π m
    c. 8.75 π m
    d. 8750 π m

34. 7130 − 2136 =

    a. 4909
    b. 4994
    c. 4494
    d. 4954

35. A woman spent 15% of her income on an item and ends up with $120. What percentage of her income is left?

    a. 12%
    b. 85%
    c. 75%
    d. 95%

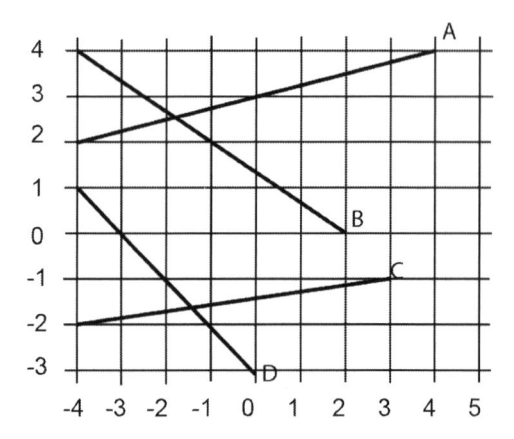

36. Which of the lines above represents the equation 2y − x = 4?

    a. A
    b. B
    c. C
    d. D

37. 1440 ÷ 12 =

    a. 122
    b. 120
    c. 110
    d. 132

5 cm

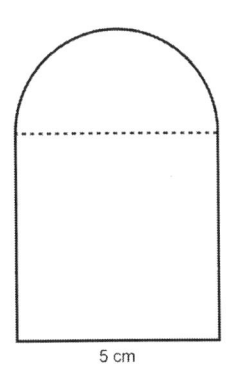

38. What is the perimeter of the above shape?

    a. 17.5 π cm
    b. 20 π cm
    c. 15 π cm
    d. 25 π cm

39. A square lawn has an area of 62,500 square meters. What is the cost of building fence around it at a rate of $5.5 per meter?

    a. $4,000
    b. $5,500
    c. $4,500
    d. $5,000

40. Solve $3^5 \div 3^8$

    a. 3^3
    b. 3^5
    c. 3^6
    d. 3^4

41. Find the sides of a right triangle whose sides are consecutive numbers.

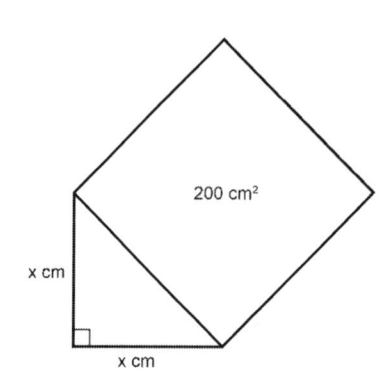

    a. 1, 2, 3
    b. 2, 3, 4
    c. 3, 4, 5
    d. 4, 5, 6

42. What is the length of the sides in the triangle above?

    a. 10
    b. 20
    c. 100
    d. 40

43. Solve the linear equation: $3(x + 2) - 2(1 - x) = 4x + 5$

    a. -1
    b. 0
    c. 1
    d. 2

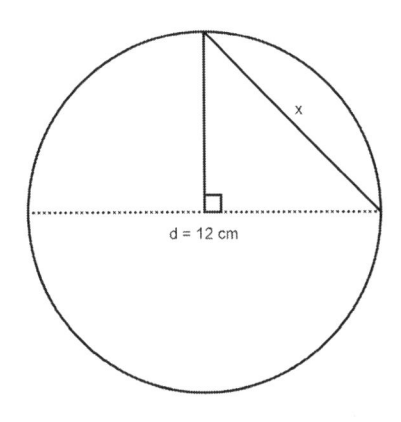

44. Calculate the length of side x.

    a. 6.46
    b. 8.46
    c. 3.6
    d. 6.4

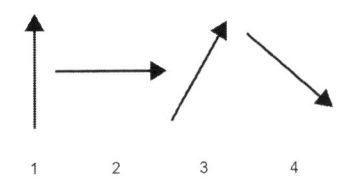

45. What is the correct order of respective slopes for the lines above?

    a. Positive, undefined, negative, positive
    b. Negative, zero, undefined, positive
    c. Undefined, zero, positive, negative
    d. Zero, positive undefined, negative

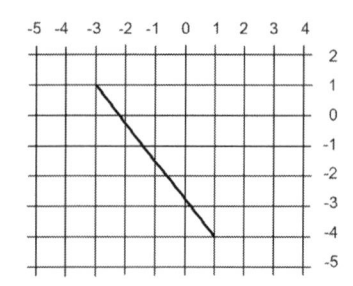

46. What is the slope of the line shown above?

a. 5/4
b. -4/5
c. -5/4
d. -4/5

47. Convert 0.045 to scientific notation.

a. 4.5×10^{-2}
b. 4.5×10^{2}
c. 4.05×10^{-2}
d. 4.5×10^{-3}

48. 5575 + 8791 =

a. 14,756
b. 14,566
c. 14,466
d. 14,366

49. A mother is 7 times older than her child. In 25 years, her age will be double that of her child. How old is the mother now?

    a. 35
    b. 33
    c. 30
    d. 25

50. In a grade 8 exam, students are asked to divide a number by 3/2, but a student mistakenly multiplied the number by 3/2 and the answer is 5 more than the required one. What was the number?

    a. 4
    b. 5
    c. 6
    d. 8

English Grammar and Usage

1. Thomas Edison _____ since he invented the light bulb, television, motion pictures, and phonograph.

    a. has always been known as the greatest inventor
    b. was always been known as the greatest inventor
    c. must have had been always known as the greatest inventor
    d. will had been known as the greatest inventor

2. Although Joe is tall for his age, his brother Elliot is _____ of the two.

    a. the tallest
    b. more tallest
    c. the tall
    d. the taller

3. When KISS came to town, all of the tickets _____ before I could buy one.

    a. will be sold out
    b. had been sold out
    c. were being sold out
    d. was sold out

4. The rules of most sports _____ more complicated than we often realize.

    a. are
    b. is
    c. was
    d. has been

5. _____ won first place in the Western Division?

    a. Who
    b. Whom
    c. Which
    d. What

6. There are now several ways to listen to music, including radio, CDs, and Mp3 files _____ you can download onto an MP3 player.

    a. on which
    b. who
    c. whom
    d. which

7. Choose the correct sentence.

a. Historians have been guessing the doctor was a woman for more than 100 years.

b. Historians have been guessing for more than 100 years the doctor was a woman.

c. Historians guessed the doctor was a woman for more than 100 years.

d. None of the above.

8. Choose the correct sentence.

a. None of us want to go to the party not even, if there will be live music.

b. None of us want to go to the party, not even if there will be live music.

c. None of us want to go to the party not even if there will be live music.

d. None of us want to go to the party; not even if there will be live music.

9. Choose the correct sentence.

a. I own two dogs, a cat named Jeffrey, and Henry, the goldfish.

b. I own two dogs a cat, named Jeffrey, and Henry, the goldfish.

c. I own two dogs, a cat named Jeffrey; and Henry, the goldfish.

d. I own two dogs, a cat, named Jeffrey and Henry, the goldfish.

10. Choose the correct sentence.

a. During the years he was President, the country fought two wars.

b. During the years he was president, the country fought two wars.

c. During the years he was president, the Country fought two wars.

d. During the years he was President, the Country fought two wars.

11. Choose the sentence with the correct grammar.

a. Don would never have thought of that book, but you could have reminded him.

b. Don would never of thought of that book, but you could have reminded him.

c. Don would never have thought of that book, but you could of have reminded him.

d. Don would never of thought of that book, but you could of reminded him.

12. Choose the correct sentence.

a. The boy and girl are related.

b. The boy and girl is related.

c. The boy and girl was related.

d. None of the above.

13. Choose the sentence with the correct grammar.

a. There was scarcely no food in the pantry, because nobody ate at home.

b. There was scarcely any food in the pantry, because nobody ate at home.

c. There was scarcely any food in the pantry, because not nobody ate at home.

d. There was scarcely no food in the pantry, because not nobody ate at home.

14. Choose the sentence with the correct grammar.

a. Its important for you to know its official name; its called the Confederate Museum.

b. It's important for you to know it's official name; it's called the Confederate Museum.

c. It's important for you to know its official name; it's called the Confederate Museum.

d. Its important for you to know it's official name; it's called the Confederate Museum.

15. Choose the sentence with the correct grammar.

a. The man as well as his son has arrived.

b. The man as well as his son have arrived.

c. Both of the above.

d. None of the above.

Essay Revision

Curiosity's Mission

Mankind's thirst for knowledge about ourselves and the universe has always been insatiable, making curiosity a driving force for human advances through history. [1] Not only that, human curiosity and creativity have created countless works of fiction that speculate about future discoveries based on the facts we know. [2]

Our neighboring planet Mars, for example, has for long lead scientists and writers to generate stories about living on the Red Planet. [3] Serious endeavors in science and technological are motivated by our never-ending questions. [4] So far, NASA has carried out several exploratory missions to Mars and the rover robot Curiosity is the latest and most sophisticated. [5]

Curiosity was launched in late November 2011 from Cape Canaveral Air Force Station in Florida. [6] It successfully landed on Mars on August 6, 2012 in search of evidence of life, if it ever existed there. [7] The car sized robot, weighing about a ton, is equipped with all the technical capacities to carry out its mission and it will be exploring our neighbor for any biological, geological and geochemical traces of life on the planet. [8] It will also try to test the Martian soil and surface to collect data about its planetary evolution and surface radiation. [9]

Curiosity has been engineered with cutting-edge technologies worth over 2.5 billion US dollars. [10] The most incredible component of the rover is the on-board science lab. [11] Apart from that, it consists of a communications system that allows transmission of commands to the rover from the control centre at NASA, enabling direct control of the robot's activities on the surface of the Red Planet. [12] The Curiosity rover has a number of mounted cameras which assists the rover to navigate as well as capture images from the Martian surface and transmit them back to Earth. [13] The rover is also designed to accommodate to the extreme conditions prevalent on Mars. [14]

1. How would you re-write sentence 1?

    a. No changes

    b. Mankind's thirst for knowledge has always been insatiable, making curiosity a driving factor for human advances through history.

    c. Mankind's thirst for knowledge is insatiable, making curiosity a driving factor for human advances through history.

    d. Humankind's thirst for knowledge is insatiable, making curiosity a driving force in advances throughout history.

2. Which sentence in the third paragraph is least relevant to the main idea of the third paragraph?

    a. 6

    b. 8

    c. 9

    d. 10

3. Which of the following is/are needed to sentence 5?

a) So far, "NASA" has carried out several exploration missions to Mars and the robot rover Curiosity is the latest and most sophisticated of all.

b) So far, NASA has carried out several exploration missions to Mars and the robot rover Curiosity is the latest and most sophisticated of all.

c) So far, NASA has carried out several exploration missions to Mars and the robot rover -Curiosity- is the latest and most sophisticated of all.

d) So far, NASA has carried out several exploration missions to Mars and the robot rover "Curiosity" is the latest and most sophisticated of all.

4. Which of the following changes is/are needed in sentence 5?

a. So far, "NASA" has carried out several exploration missions to Mars and the rover robot Curiosity is the latest and most sophisticated of all.

b. So far, NASA has carried out several exploratory missions to Mars and the rover robot Curiosity is the latest and most sophisticated of all.

c. So far, NASA has carried out several exploration missions to Mars and the rover robot -Curiosity- is the latest and most sophisticated of all.

d. So far, NASA has carried out several exploratory missions to Mars and the rover robot "Curiosity" is the latest and most sophisticated of all.

Green Energy from Olive Oil

The debate about developing sustainable energy sources have been very active over the past two decades.[1] With continued concern over global climate change, environmentalists are urging governments for lowering their dependence on fossil fuels in order for ensuring reduced carbon emission into the atmosphere.[2] Consequently, governments worldwide are turning their attention to the search for non-emissive sources of energy. [3] Renewable substitutes under extensive research are solar power, wind, geothermal energy and harnessing energy from ocean waves. [4]

While the search for environment friendly energy sources is already under way, developing these alternatives at a reasonable cost is a major challenge. [5] No cost-effective replacement for fossil fuels has yet been found. [6] However, recent years have seen remarkable progress in the field of solar energy. [7] Ted Sargent, a Professor at University of Toronto, Canada, has discovered that olive oil has the capacity to capture solar radiation and emit electrons resulting in an electric current. [8] This major discovery in the solar power generation industry as it offers a cheap source of harnessing the Sun's energy. [9]

Oleic acid, the main ingredient of olive oil, absorbs infrared radiation is the major component of the Sun's radiation reaching the Earth. [10] The discovery is significant because so far, no attempt has been made to use the abundant infrared radiation we receive throughout the year. [11] Infrared (IR) light is electromagnetic radiation with longer wavelengths than those of visible light. [12] Capturing this heat wave radiation, along with the photons that are present in sunlight, increases the efficiency of the solar cells that are already being manufactured commercially. [13] And to make it possible, Professor Sargent has developed a new kind of solar cell called "quantum dots," tiny cells made from gels of tin, bismuth, lead, sulphur and selenium mixed with extra pure olive oil. [14] The resulting ink-like crystal absorbs both photons and infrared radiation and has the capacity to transmit electrons and produce a current. [15]

This new method of capturing the Sun's energy is considered a breakthrough in the solar power industry as it offers cheaper alternatives to the existing use of silicon crystals which are costly to manufacture. [16] And although the invention is yet to prove it's efficiency in harnessing solar energy, alot of funding has already been dedicated to further research. [17]

5. What sentence is not related to the main idea of paragraph 2?

    a. 6

    b. 10

    c. 12

    d. 13

6. Which of the following is a correct version of sentence 17?

    a. And although the invention is yet to prove its efficiency in harnessing solar energy, alot of funding has already been dedicated to further research.

    b. And although the invention is yet to prove it's efficiency in harnessing solar energy, a lot of funding has already been dedicated to further research.

    c. And although the invention is yet to prove its efficiency in harnessing solar energy, a lot of funding has already been dedicated to further research.

    d. No changes are necessary.

7. Which of the following changes are needed in sentence 10?

    a. Oleic acid, the main ingredient of olive oil, absorbs infrared radiation is the major component of the Sun's radiation reaching the Earth.

    b. Oleic acid, the main ingredient of olive oil, absorbs infrared radiation, which is the major component of the Sun's radiation reaching the Earth.

    c. Oleic acid, the main ingredient of olive oil absorbs infrared radiation that is the major component of the Sun's radiation reaching the Earth.

    d. Oleic acid, the main ingredient of olive oil, absorbs infrared radiation what is the major component of the Sun's radiation reaching the Earth.

8. Which of the following changes are needed in sentence 2?

a. With continued concern over global climate change, environmentalists are urging governments to lowering their dependence on fossil fuels to ensuring reduced carbon emission into the atmosphere.

b. With continued concern over global climate change, environmentalists are urging governments lower their dependence on fossil fuels in order for ensuring reduced carbon emission into the atmosphere.

c. With continued concern over global climate change, environmentalists are urging governments to lower their dependence on fossil fuels in order for ensuring reduced carbon emission into the atmosphere.

d. With continued concern over global climate change, environmentalists are urging governments to lower their dependence on fossil fuels to ensure reduced carbon emission into the atmosphere.

Hunting Lost Cities from Space

Satellite imaging has become widespread with improvements in telecommunication over the past two decades. [1] Communication satellites in orbit around the Earth have enabled large-scale mapping of the planet's surface which has become freely available thanks to technology giants like Google. [2] Satellite mapping has opened up new possibilities in diverse fields of science and technology. [3]

The key feature of the new tool, according to Professor Sarah Parcak, who discovered many cities, temples and pyramids covered under sands and sediment; is that it offers a wider perspective in size and scale of the location under study. [4] Along with the visual information that the satellite images provide, numerous details about the sites can be obtained from infrared (IR) and gravitational field images. [5] This information, coupled with conventional on-site procedures, are vital for archeology. [6]

IR data collected from satellite imaging provide clues about the activities of humans living in the contemporary times of their civilizations- including their agriculture, vegetation, structures, habitation roads and much more. [7] This type of information is derived from IR imagery which detects IR radiation present in sunlight as it is reflected by the Earth. [8] Different points in a civilization reflect IR radiation in different proportions, revealing the contrast between different areas and provide detailed insight about the causes of these differing heat signatures. [9]

9. Which of the following changes in sentence 6 would focus attention on the main idea of the second paragraph?

    a. These information, along with a supply of some heavy machinery, will help the excavation of every archeological site accomplished within a short period of time.

    b. This information, coupled with conventional on-site procedures, help archeologists plan their excavation carefully and efficiently.

    c. Such details are valuable records of ancient history and are essential assets of any civilization.

    d. Such details, unfortunately, are available to archeological firms who are willing to invest a lot of money on putting satellites into orbit.

10. What is the best way to re-write the underlined portion of sentence 6?

    a. coupled
    b. together with
    c. and
    d. or

11. Which of the following sentences, if inserted after sentence 3, would best illustrate the main idea of the passage?

    a. The application has inspired archeologists to use it for searching for the traces of ancient civilizations and other anthropological dynamics.

    b. The new technology will be very useful for excavation of archeological sites.

    c. The application is a breakthrough for archeology and anthropology since it will allows us to zoom into the distant past to look for lost civilizations.

    d. The concept has many positive aspects in the field of archeological science and excavation.

12. Which of the following change(s) is/are needed to sentence 4?

    a. The key feature of the new tool- according to Professor Sarah Parcak, who discovered many cities, temples and pyramids covered under sands and sediment- is that it offers a wider perspective in size and scale of the location.

    b. The key feature of the new tool- according to Professor Sarah Parcak- who discovered many cities, temples and pyramids covered under sands and sediment, is that it offers a wider perspective in size and scale of the location under study.

    c. The key feature of the new tool according to Professor Sarah Parcak- who discovered many cities, temples and pyramids covered under sands and sediment- is that it offers a wider perspective in size and scale of the location under study.

    d. The key feature of the new tool, according to Professor Sarah Parcak- who discovered many cities, temples and pyramids covered under sands and sediment is that it offers a wider perspective in size and scale of the location under study.

Answer Key

Reading

1. B
We can infer from this passage that sickness from an infectious disease can be easily transmitted from one person to another.

From the passage, "Infectious pathologies are also called communicable diseases or transmissible diseases, due to their potential of transmission from one person or species to another by a replicating agent (as opposed to a toxin)."

2. A
Two other names for infectious pathologies are communicable diseases and transmissible diseases.

From the passage, "Infectious pathologies are also called communicable diseases or transmissible diseases, due to their potential of transmission from one person or species to another by a replicating agent (as opposed to a toxin)."

3. C
Infectivity describes the ability of an organism to enter, survive and multiply in the host. This is taken directly from the passage, and is a definition type question.

Definition type questions can be answered quickly and easily by scanning the passage for the word you are asked to define.

"Infectivity" is an unusual word, so it is quick and easy to scan the passage looking for this word.

4. B
We know an infection is not synonymous with an infectious disease because an infection may not cause important clinical symptoms or impair host function.

5. C
The cumulus stage of a thunderstorm is the beginning of the

thunderstorm.

This is taken directly from the passage, "The first stage of a thunderstorm is the cumulus, or developing stage."

6. D
The passage lists four ways that air is heated. One of the ways is, heat created by water vapor condensing into liquid.

7. A
The sequence of events can be taken from these sentences:

As the moisture carried by the [1] air currents rises, it rapidly cools into liquid drops of water, which appear as cumulus clouds. As the water vapor condenses into liquid, it [2] releases heat, which warms the air. This in turn causes the air to become less dense than the surrounding dry air and [3] rise further.

8. C
The purpose of this text is to explain when meteorologists consider a thunderstorm severe.

The main idea is the first sentence, "The United States National Weather Service classifies thunderstorms as severe when they reach a predetermined level." After the first sentence, the passage explains and elaborates on this idea. Everything is this passage is related to this idea, and there are no other major ideas in this passage that are central to the whole passage.

9. A
From this passage, we can infer that different areas and countries have different criteria for determining a severe storm.

From the passage we can see that most of the US has a criteria of, winds over 50 knots (58 mph or 93 km/h), and hail ¾ inch (2 cm). For the Central US, hail must be 1 inch (2.5 cm) in diameter. In Canada, winds must be 90 km/h or greater, hail 2 centimeters in diameter or greater, and rainfall more than 50 millimeters in 1 hour, or 75 millimeters in 3 hours.

Option D is incorrect because the Canadian system is the same for hail, 2 centimeters in diameter.

10. C
With hail above the minimum size of 2.5 cm. diameter, the Central Region of the United States National Weather Service would issue a severe thunderstorm warning.

11. C
You would find information about natural selection and adaptation in the ecology section which begins on page 110.

12. D
Clouds in space are made of different materials attracted by gravity. Clouds on Earth are made of water droplets or ice crystals.

Choice D is the best answer. Notice also that Choice D is the most specific.

13. C
The main idea is the first sentence of the passage; a cloud is a visible mass of droplets or frozen crystals floating in the atmosphere above the surface of the Earth or other planetary body.

The main idea is very often the first sentence of the paragraph.

14. C
This question asks about the process, and gives options that can be confirmed or eliminated easily.

From the passage, "Dense, deep clouds reflect most light, so they appear white, at least from the top. Cloud droplets scatter light very efficiently, so the further into a cloud light travels, the weaker it gets. This accounts for the gray or dark appearance at the base of large clouds."

We can eliminate choice A, since water droplets inside the cloud do not reflect light is false.

We can eliminate choice B, since, water droplets outside the cloud reflect light, it appears dark, is false.

Choice C is correct.

15. A
The correct order of ingredients is brown sugar, baking soda and chocolate chips.

16. B
Sturdy: strong, solid in structure or person. In context, Stir in chocolate chips by hand with a *sturdy* wooden spoon.

17. A
Disperse: to scatter in different directions or break up. In context, Stir until the chocolate chips and nuts are evenly *dispersed*.

18. B
You can stop stirring the nuts when they are evenly distributed. From the passage, "Stir until the chocolate chips and nuts are evenly dispersed."

19. B
Reading the document posted to the Human Resources website is optional.

20. B
The document is recommended changes and have not be implemented yet.

21. A
Navy SEALS are the maritime component of the United States Special Operations Command (USSOCOM).

22. C
Working underwater separates SEALs from other military units. This is taken directly from the passage.

Practice Test Questions 1 65

23. D
SEALs also belong to the Navy and the Coast Guard.

24. A
The CIA also participated. From the passage, the raid was conducted by a "team of 40 *CIA-led* Navy SEALS."

25. C
From the passage, "The Navy SEALs were part of the Naval Special Warfare Development Group, previously called "Team 6". "

26. A
The sentence is a recommendation.

27. C
Tips for a good night's sleep is the best alternative title for this article.

28. B
Mental activity is helpful for a good night's sleep is can not be inferred from this article.

29. A
The Save the Children's fund has raised $12,000 out of $20,000, or 12/20. Simplifying, 12/20 = 3/5

30. B
The Save the Children's fund has raised $12,000 out of $16,000, or 12/16. Simplifying, 12/16 = 3/4

Mathematics

1. C
9,177 + 7,204 = 1973

2. C
If there are 5 friends and each drink costs $1.89, we can round up to $2 per drink and estimate the total cost at, 5 X $2 = $10.
The actual, cost is 5 X $1.89 = $9.45.

3. A
643 - 587 =

4. C
243/3 x 3 x 3 = 243/27 = 9

5. A
The graph shows oil consumption peaked in 2011.

6. D
If we subtract 25 pounds from the total 205, then in remaining 180 pounds, their weights are equal. So Sarah's weight will be = 90 + 25 = 115 pounds.

In kilograms it will be = 115×0.4535 = 52.15 Kg.
Sarah will weigh approximately 52 Kg.

7. B
The line is pointing towards numbers less than 1. The equation is therefore, X < 1.

8. B
(14 + 2) x 2 + 3 = 35. Order or operations, do brackets first, then multiplication and division, then addition and subtraction.

9. D
75/1500 = 15/300 = 3/60 = 1/20

10. B
(3, 3)
2x + 3 = y + 6
-4x - 12 = -8y

y = 2x + 3 - 6
y = 2x - 3
-4x - 12 = -8(2x - 3)
-4x - 12 = -16x + 24
-4x + 16 = 12 + 24
12x = 36
x = 3

y = 2x - 3
y = 2 * 3 - 3 = 3

11. A
491 ÷ 9 = 54 r5

12. B

Day	Number of Absent Students	Number of Present Students	% Attendance
Monday	5	40	88.88%
Tuesday	9	36	80.00%
Wednesday	4	41	91.11%
Thursday	10	35	77.77%
Friday	6	39	86.66%

To find the average or mean, sum the series and divide by the number of items.
88.88 + 80.00 + 91.11 + 77.77 + 86.66/5
424.42/5 = 84.88
Round up to 85%.

Percentage attendance will be 85%

13. C
Let the original price be x, then at the rate of 7% the discounted price will be = 0.93x. 2% discounted amount then will be = 0.02 × 0.93x = 0.0186x. Remaining price=0.93x - 0.0186x = 0.9114x. This is the amount which John has paid so 0.9114x = 425. X = 425/0.9114. Solving for X = 466.31

14. D
Comparing angles on similar triangles, a, b and c will be 70°, 35°, 35°

15. B
(7 x 7 x 7 x 7 x 7 x 7) - (10 x 10 x 10) = 16,807 – 1,000 = 15,807.

16. C
To find the perimeter of an equilateral triangle with 9 cm. sides, add the sides. 9+9+9 = 27 cm.

17. A
Yes the triangles are congruent. This is a case of SSA:

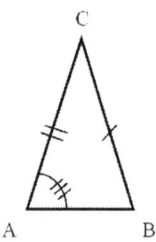

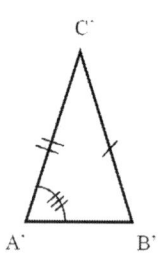

18. A
The scientific notation is in the positive so we shift the decimal 6 places to the right. Thus it is 5,630,000

19. B
4y + 24 = 3y + 30, = 4y − 3y + 24 = 30, = y + 24 = 30, = y = 30 − 24, = y = 6

20. C
10 x 2 − (7 + 9) = 4. This is an order of operations question. Do brackets first, then multiplication and division, then addition and subtraction.

21. C
1 inch on map = 2,000 inches on ground. So 5.2 inches on map = 5.2 x 2,000 = 10,440 inches on ground.

22. D
Perimeter of triangle ABC within two squares.
Perimeter = sum of the sides.
Perimeter = 8.5 + 8.5 + 6 + 6
Perimeter = 29 cm.

23. A
10 x 10 x 100 x 100 = 1000^x, =100 x 10,000 = 1000^x, = 1,000,000 = 1000^x = x =2

24. B
a + b + c + d = ?
The sum of angles around a point is 360°
a + b + c + d = 360°

25. A
5^6

26. C
1278 + 4920 = 6198

27. B
Actual cost = X, therefore, 545 = x + 0.15x, 545 = 1x + 0.15x, 545 = 1.15x, x = 545/1.15 = 473.9

28. C
Exponential form is 9^3 and standard from is 729

29. D
First convert the units to grams. Since 1000 g = 1 kg, 10 kg = 10 x 1000 = 10,000 + 550 g = 10,550 g. Divide 10,550 among 5 = 10550/5 = 2110 = 2 kg 110 g

30. C
0.524/ 10 x 10 x 10 = 0.524/1000 = 0.000524

31. D
5x/2 = 3x + 24/6
3 * 5x/3 * 2 = 3x + 24/6
15x/6 = 3x + 24/6
15x = 3x + 24
15x - 3x = 25
12x = 24
x = 24/12 = 2

32. D
When multiplying exponents with the same base, add the exponents. 3^2 x 3^5 = 3^{2+5} = 3^7

33. A
Diameter = 2 x radius.
Circumference = π x Diameter

Distance(meters) = (Circumference x Revolutions)/100
Distance(meters) = [((25 x 2) π) x 175]/100
Distance(meters) = 8750 π/100
Distance = 87.5 π meters.

34. B
7130 − 2136 = 4994

35. B
She spent 15% - 100% - 15% = 85%

36. A
Line A represents the equation 2y − x = 4.

37. B
1440 ÷ 12 = 120

38. A
The shape is made of a square and a semi circle. Calculate the perimeter of each and add.
Perimeter = 3 sides of the square + ½ circumference of the circle.
= (3 x 5) + ½(5 π)
= 15 + 2.5 π
Perimeter = 17.5 π cm

39. B
As the lawn is square, the length of one side will be = √62,500 = 250 meters. So the perimeters will be 250 × 4 = 1000 meters. The total cost will be 1000 × 5.5 = $5500.

40. A
To divide exponents with the same base, subtract the exponents. $3^{8-5} = 3^3$

41. C
The length of the sides is, 3, 4, 5.
x
y = x + 1
z = x + 2
$x^2 + y^2 = y^2$
$x^2 + (x + 1)^2 = (x + 2)^2$
$x^2 + x^2 + 2x + 1 = x^2 + 4x + 4$
$x^2 - 2x - 3$ 0

$x_{1,2} = 2 \pm \sqrt{4 + 12} \;/\; 2$
$x_{1,2} = 2 \pm 4 \;/\; 2$

x = 3
y = 4
z = 5

42. A
Pythagorean Theorem:
(Hypotenuse)^2 = (Perpendicular)^2 + (Base)^2
$h^2 = a^2 + b^2$

Given: $h^2 = 200$, a = b = x
Then, $x^2 + x^2 = 200$, $2x^2 = 200$, $x^2 = 100$
x = 10

43. C
3(x + 2) - 2(1 - x) = 4x + 5
3x + 6 - 2 + 2x = 4x + 5
5x + 4 = 4x + 5
5x - 4x = 5 - 4
x = 1

44. B
Pythagorean Theorem:
(Hypotenuse)^2 = (Perpendicular)^2 + (Base)^2
$h^2 = a^2 + b^2$

Given: d (diameter)= 12 & r (radius) = a = b = 6
$h^2 = a^2 + b^2$
$h^2 = 6^2 + 6^2$, $h^2 = 36 + 36$
$h^2 = 72$
h = 8.46

45. C
Undefined, zero, positive, negative.

46. C
Slope (m) = $\dfrac{\text{change in y}}{\text{change in x}}$

$(x_1, y_1)=(-3,1)$ & $(x_2, y_2)= (1,-4)$
Slope = [-4 - 1]/[1-(-3)]= -5/4

47. A
The decimal point moves 2 spaces to the left to be placed

after 4, which is the first non-zero number. 4.5 x 10^{-2} The exponent is negation since the decimal moved left.

48. D
5575 + 8791 = 14366

49. A
Suppose mother's age is x years and the child's is y. Then y = 7x. After 25 years, y + 25 = 2(x + 25). Solving for y, y + 25 = 2x + 50. Putting the value of y = 7x in the below equation 7x + 25 = 2x + 50. Solving for x = 5 years. So child is 5 years old and mother is 35.

50. C
Let the number be x. (x * 3/2) – (x / 3/2) = 5
X = 6

English Grammar and Usage

1. A
The sentence requires the past perfect "has always been known." This is the only grammatically correct choice.

2. D
When comparing two items, use "the taller." When comparing more than two items, use "the tallest."

3. B
The past perfect form is used to describe an event that occurred in the past and prior to another event. Here there are two things that happened, both of them in the past, and something the person wanted to do.

Event 1: Kiss came to town
Event 2: All the tickets sold out
What I wanted to do: Buy a ticket

The events are arranged:
When KISS came to town, all of the tickets **had been sold out** before I could buy one.

4. A
The subject is "rules" so the present tense plural form, "are,"

is used to agree with "realize."

5. A
"Who" is correct because the question uses an active construction. "To whom was first place given?" is a passive construction.

6. D
"Which" is correct, because the files are objects and not people.

7. B
The correct sentence is
Historians have been guessing for more than 100 years the doctor was a woman.

Here the phrase 'for more than 100 years' refers to how long historians have been guessing, and not to how long the doctor has been a woman.

8. B
Use a comma separates independent clauses. None of us wants to go to the party, not even if there will be live music.

9. A
This is an example where a comma appears before 'and,' but is disambiguating. Without the comma, the sentence would be "I own two dogs, a cat named Jeffrey and Henry, the goldfish." This means there is a cat named Jeffrey and Henry, and a goldfish with no name mentioned. The comma appears to show the distinction.

I own two dogs, a cat named Jeffrey, and Henry, the goldfish.

10. B
President is not capitalized unless used with a name as in, President Obama.

11. A
The third conditional is used for talking about an unreal situation (a situation that did not happen) in the past. For example, "If I had studied harder, [if clause] I would have

passed the exam" [main clause]. This has the same meaning as, "I failed the exam, because I didn't study hard enough."

12. A
Use a plural verb form for two subjects linked by "and."

13. B
In double negative sentences, one of the negatives is replaced with "any."

14. C
"It's" is a contraction for it is or it has. "Its" is a possessive pronoun.

15. A
When two subjects are linked by "with" or "as well," use the verb form that matches the first subject.

Essay Revision

1. D
Suggested revision of sentence 1, "Humankind's thirst for knowledge is insatiable, making curiosity a driving force for advances throughout history."

Use the gender neutral "humankind. Replace the past perfect "has always been" with the present tense to make a simpler and more direct sentence. "Though history" is incorrect. Use "throughout" when referring to a time period. Replace the preposition "for" with "in."

2. A
Sentence 6 is the least relevant. "Curiosity was launched in late November 2011 from Cape Canaveral Air Force Station in Florida."

The third paragraph talks about the objectives of the rover. All sentences other than sentence 7 mention the objectives. This sentence, however, informs about when the spacecraft was launched.

3. D
Suggested changes to sentence 5, "So far, NASA has carried

out several exploration missions to Mars and the robot rover "Curiosity" is the latest and most sophisticated of all."

"Curiosity" is the name of a spacecraft that was assigned the particular name because of its association of its mission to satisfy our curiosity about the planet Mars. In this respect, the name bears a special meaning and emphasis which must be reflected in representing it using the quotation mark. In this case, only option D offers this change.

4. D
The changes needed to sentence 5 are, "So far, NASA has carried out several exploratory missions to Mars and the rover robot "Curiosity" is the latest and most sophisticated of all."

"Curiosity" is the name of a spacecraft that was assigned the particular name because of its association of its mission to satisfy our curiosity about the planet Mars. In this respect, the name bears a special meaning and emphasis, which must be reflected in representing it using the quotation mark.

Use of the adjective "exploratory" to describe the missions is correct.

Option D offers these changes.

5. C
Sentence 12, which talks about infrared light is not relevant to the main idea of paragraph 2.

6. C
And although the invention is yet to prove its efficiency in harnessing solar energy, a lot of funding has already been dedicated to further research.

Option C has the correct use of "its" and "a lot."

7. B
Suggested corrections to sentence 10, "Oleic acid, the main ingredient of olive oil, absorbs infra-red radiation, which is the major component of the Sun's radiation reaching the Earth."

The sentence is missing the subordinate conjunction "which" or "that" necessary to construct the subordinate clause, with a comma before "which." Options B and C suggest these changes, but since option C contains a punctuation error, only B is has the valid answer.

8. D
Suggested changes to sentence 2, "With continued concern over global climate change, environmentalists are urging governments to lower their dependence on fossil fuels to ensure reduced carbon emission into the atmosphere."

This sentence contains inappropriate use of gerunds and infinitives. To-infinitives are preferred when the continuous form of a main verb is used right before or after them. In this case, "urging" should be followed by the to-infinitive of "lower". Further across the sentence, the linking phrase "to", has only one acceptable form; itself. Therefore, the verb which is linked to must contain the infinitive form. The gerund form must be discarded. The only valid option is D.

9. B
"This information, coupled with conventional on-site procedures, help archeologists plan their excavation carefully and efficiently."

The second paragraph points out the significance of satellite imaging for archeological studies. The original sentence only makes a general claim. Option A contradicts excavation principles by adding "along with a supply of heavy machinery" which would destroy the site. Option B, more appropriately, adds the aspects of archeological excavation that are going to be boosted by the technology. Options C and D offer very little relevance to satellite imaging and the dimensions of excavation that are going to be affected.

10. B
The underlined portion of sentence 6, "coupled with" can be re-written as, "together with."

11. A
The following sentence, inserted after sentence 3, would

best illustrate the main idea, "The application has inspired archeologists to use it for searching for the traces of ancient civilizations and other anthropological dynamics."

Option A points out the significance of the application with some details that are addressed in the subsequent paragraphs. All other options are either too general or less relevant to the main idea of the passage.

12. A
Suggested changes to sentence 4 are, "The key feature of the new tool- according to Professor Sarah Parcak, who discovered many cities, temples and pyramids covered under sands and sediment- is that it offers a wider perspective in size and scale of the location."

The changes in this sentence are related to punctuation. The original sentence contains a semicolon before a verbal phrase which is not justifiable with its standard use. The sentence can be modified using parenthetic dashes as using parenthetic commas make the sentence very complicated since there are several clauses and a list. Option A has the valid answer only.

Practice Test Questions Set 2

The questions below are not the same as you will find on the CAHSEE® - that would be too easy! And nobody knows what the questions will be and they change all the time. Below are general questions that cover the same subject areas as the CAHSEE®. So, while the format and exact wording of the questions may differ slightly, and change from year to year, if you can answer the questions below, you will have no problem with the CAHSEE®.

For the best results, take these Practice Test Questions as if it were the real exam. Set aside time when you will not be disturbed, and a location that is quiet and free of distractions. Read the instructions carefully, read each question carefully, and answer to the best of your ability.
Use the bubble answer sheets provided. When you have completed the Practice Questions, check your answer against the Answer Key and read the explanation provided.

Do not attempt more than one set of practice test questions in one day. After completing the first practice test, wait two or three days before attempting the second set of questions.

Reading Answer Sheet

1. Ⓐ Ⓑ Ⓒ Ⓓ   11. Ⓐ Ⓑ Ⓒ Ⓓ   21. Ⓐ Ⓑ Ⓒ Ⓓ
2. Ⓐ Ⓑ Ⓒ Ⓓ   12. Ⓐ Ⓑ Ⓒ Ⓓ   22. Ⓐ Ⓑ Ⓒ Ⓓ
3. Ⓐ Ⓑ Ⓒ Ⓓ   13. Ⓐ Ⓑ Ⓒ Ⓓ   23. Ⓐ Ⓑ Ⓒ Ⓓ
4. Ⓐ Ⓑ Ⓒ Ⓓ   14. Ⓐ Ⓑ Ⓒ Ⓓ   24. Ⓐ Ⓑ Ⓒ Ⓓ
5. Ⓐ Ⓑ Ⓒ Ⓓ   15. Ⓐ Ⓑ Ⓒ Ⓓ   25. Ⓐ Ⓑ Ⓒ Ⓓ
6. Ⓐ Ⓑ Ⓒ Ⓓ   16. Ⓐ Ⓑ Ⓒ Ⓓ   26. Ⓐ Ⓑ Ⓒ Ⓓ
7. Ⓐ Ⓑ Ⓒ Ⓓ   17. Ⓐ Ⓑ Ⓒ Ⓓ   27. Ⓐ Ⓑ Ⓒ Ⓓ
8. Ⓐ Ⓑ Ⓒ Ⓓ   18. Ⓐ Ⓑ Ⓒ Ⓓ   28. Ⓐ Ⓑ Ⓒ Ⓓ
9. Ⓐ Ⓑ Ⓒ Ⓓ   19. Ⓐ Ⓑ Ⓒ Ⓓ   29. Ⓐ Ⓑ Ⓒ Ⓓ
10. Ⓐ Ⓑ Ⓒ Ⓓ   20. Ⓐ Ⓑ Ⓒ Ⓓ   30. Ⓐ Ⓑ Ⓒ Ⓓ

Mathematics Answer Sheet

1. Ⓐ Ⓑ Ⓒ Ⓓ
2. Ⓐ Ⓑ Ⓒ Ⓓ
3. Ⓐ Ⓑ Ⓒ Ⓓ
4. Ⓐ Ⓑ Ⓒ Ⓓ
5. Ⓐ Ⓑ Ⓒ Ⓓ
6. Ⓐ Ⓑ Ⓒ Ⓓ
7. Ⓐ Ⓑ Ⓒ Ⓓ
8. Ⓐ Ⓑ Ⓒ Ⓓ
9. Ⓐ Ⓑ Ⓒ Ⓓ
10. Ⓐ Ⓑ Ⓒ Ⓓ
11. Ⓐ Ⓑ Ⓒ Ⓓ
12. Ⓐ Ⓑ Ⓒ Ⓓ
13. Ⓐ Ⓑ Ⓒ Ⓓ
14. Ⓐ Ⓑ Ⓒ Ⓓ
15. Ⓐ Ⓑ Ⓒ Ⓓ
16. Ⓐ Ⓑ Ⓒ Ⓓ
17. Ⓐ Ⓑ Ⓒ Ⓓ

18. Ⓐ Ⓑ Ⓒ Ⓓ
19. Ⓐ Ⓑ Ⓒ Ⓓ
20. Ⓐ Ⓑ Ⓒ Ⓓ
21. Ⓐ Ⓑ Ⓒ Ⓓ
22. Ⓐ Ⓑ Ⓒ Ⓓ
23. Ⓐ Ⓑ Ⓒ Ⓓ
24. Ⓐ Ⓑ Ⓒ Ⓓ
25. Ⓐ Ⓑ Ⓒ Ⓓ
26. Ⓐ Ⓑ Ⓒ Ⓓ
27. Ⓐ Ⓑ Ⓒ Ⓓ
28. Ⓐ Ⓑ Ⓒ Ⓓ
29. Ⓐ Ⓑ Ⓒ Ⓓ
30. Ⓐ Ⓑ Ⓒ Ⓓ
31. Ⓐ Ⓑ Ⓒ Ⓓ
32. Ⓐ Ⓑ Ⓒ Ⓓ
33. Ⓐ Ⓑ Ⓒ Ⓓ
34. Ⓐ Ⓑ Ⓒ Ⓓ

35. Ⓐ Ⓑ Ⓒ Ⓓ
36. Ⓐ Ⓑ Ⓒ Ⓓ
37. Ⓐ Ⓑ Ⓒ Ⓓ
38. Ⓐ Ⓑ Ⓒ Ⓓ
39. Ⓐ Ⓑ Ⓒ Ⓓ
40. Ⓐ Ⓑ Ⓒ Ⓓ
41. Ⓐ Ⓑ Ⓒ Ⓓ
42. Ⓐ Ⓑ Ⓒ Ⓓ
43. Ⓐ Ⓑ Ⓒ Ⓓ
44. Ⓐ Ⓑ Ⓒ Ⓓ
45. Ⓐ Ⓑ Ⓒ Ⓓ
46. Ⓐ Ⓑ Ⓒ Ⓓ
47. Ⓐ Ⓑ Ⓒ Ⓓ
48. Ⓐ Ⓑ Ⓒ Ⓓ
49. Ⓐ Ⓑ Ⓒ Ⓓ
50. Ⓐ Ⓑ Ⓒ Ⓓ

Essay Revision - English Grammar and Usage Answer Sheet

1. Ⓐ Ⓑ Ⓒ Ⓓ 11. Ⓐ Ⓑ Ⓒ Ⓓ 21. Ⓐ Ⓑ Ⓒ Ⓓ

2. Ⓐ Ⓑ Ⓒ Ⓓ 12. Ⓐ Ⓑ Ⓒ Ⓓ 22. Ⓐ Ⓑ Ⓒ Ⓓ

3. Ⓐ Ⓑ Ⓒ Ⓓ 13. Ⓐ Ⓑ Ⓒ Ⓓ 23. Ⓐ Ⓑ Ⓒ Ⓓ

4. Ⓐ Ⓑ Ⓒ Ⓓ 14. Ⓐ Ⓑ Ⓒ Ⓓ 24. Ⓐ Ⓑ Ⓒ Ⓓ

5. Ⓐ Ⓑ Ⓒ Ⓓ 15. Ⓐ Ⓑ Ⓒ Ⓓ 25. Ⓐ Ⓑ Ⓒ Ⓓ

6. Ⓐ Ⓑ Ⓒ Ⓓ 16. Ⓐ Ⓑ Ⓒ Ⓓ 26. Ⓐ Ⓑ Ⓒ Ⓓ

7. Ⓐ Ⓑ Ⓒ Ⓓ 17. Ⓐ Ⓑ Ⓒ Ⓓ 27. Ⓐ Ⓑ Ⓒ Ⓓ

8. Ⓐ Ⓑ Ⓒ Ⓓ 18. Ⓐ Ⓑ Ⓒ Ⓓ 28. Ⓐ Ⓑ Ⓒ Ⓓ

9. Ⓐ Ⓑ Ⓒ Ⓓ 19. Ⓐ Ⓑ Ⓒ Ⓓ 29. Ⓐ Ⓑ Ⓒ Ⓓ

10. Ⓐ Ⓑ Ⓒ Ⓓ 20. Ⓐ Ⓑ Ⓒ Ⓓ 30. Ⓐ Ⓑ Ⓒ Ⓓ

Part 1 – Reading and Language Arts

Questions 1-4 refer to the following passage.

The Respiratory System

The respiratory system's function is to allow oxygen exchange through all parts of the body. The anatomy or structure of the exchange system, and the uses of the exchanged gases, varies depending on the organism. In humans and other mammals, for example, the anatomical features of the respiratory system include airways, lungs, and the respiratory muscles. Molecules of oxygen and carbon dioxide are passively exchanged, by diffusion, between the gaseous external environment and the blood. This exchange process occurs in the alveolar region of the lungs.

Other animals, such as insects, have respiratory systems with very simple anatomical features, and in amphibians even the skin plays a vital role in gas exchange. Plants also have respiratory systems but the direction of gas exchange can be opposite to that of animals.

The respiratory system can also be divided into physiological, or functional, zones. These include the conducting zone (the region for gas transport from the outside atmosphere to just above the alveoli), the transitional zone, and the respiratory zone (the alveolar region where gas exchange occurs). [6]

1. What can we infer from the first paragraph in this passage?

    a. Human and mammal respiratory systems are the same

    b. The lungs are an important part of the respiratory system

    c. The respiratory system varies in different mammals

    d. Oxygen and carbon dioxide are passive exchanged by the respiratory system

2. What is the process by which molecules of oxygen and carbon dioxide are passively exchanged?

    a. Transfusion

    b. Affusion

    c. Diffusion

    d. Respiratory confusion

3. What organ plays an important role in gas exchange in amphibians?

    a. The skin

    b. The lungs

    c. The gills

    d. The mouth

4. What are the three physiological zones of the respiratory system?

    a. Conducting, transitional, respiratory zones

    b. Redacting, transitional, circulatory zones

    c. Conducting, circulatory, inhibiting zones

    d. Transitional, inhibiting, conducting zones

Questions 5-8 refer to the following passage.

ABC Electric Warranty

ABC Electric Company warrants that its products are free from defects in material and workmanship. Subject to the conditions and limitations set forth below, ABC Electric will, at its option, either repair or replace any part of its products that prove defective due to improper workmanship or materials.

This limited warranty does not cover any damage to the product from improper installation, accident, abuse, misuse, natural disaster, insufficient or excessive electrical supply, abnormal mechanical or environmental conditions, or any unauthorized disassembly, repair, or modification.

This limited warranty also does not apply to any product on which the original identification information has been altered, or removed, has not been handled or packaged correctly, or has been sold as second-hand.

This limited warranty covers only repair, replacement, refund or credit for defective ABC Electric products, as provided above.

5. I tried to repair my ABC Electric blender, but could not, so can I get it repaired under this warranty?

    a. Yes, the warranty still covers the blender

    b. No, the warranty does not cover the blender

    c. Uncertain. ABC Electric may or may not cover repairs under this warranty

6. My ABC Electric fan is not working. Will ABC Electric provide a new one or repair this one?

    a. ABC Electric will repair my fan

    b. ABC Electric will replace my fan

    c. ABC Electric could either replace or repair my fan

    I can request either a replacement or a repair.

7. My stove was damaged in a flood. Does this warranty cover my stove?

    a. Yes, it is covered.

    b. No, it is not covered.

    c. It may or may not be covered.

    d. ABC Electric will decide if it is covered

8. Which of the following is an example of improper workmanship?

    a. Missing parts

    b. Defective parts

    c. Scratches on the front

    d. None of the above

Questions 9 - 12 refer to the following passage.

Low Blood Sugar

As the name suggest, low blood sugar is low sugar levels in the bloodstream. This can occur when you have not eaten properly and undertake strenuous activity, or when you are very hungry. When Low blood sugar occurs regularly and is ongoing, it is a medical condition called hypoglycemia. This condition can occur in diabetics and also in healthy adults.

Causes of low blood sugar can include excessive alcohol consumption, metabolic problems, stomach surgery, pancreas, liver or kidneys problems, as well as a side-effect of some medications.

Symptoms

There are different symptoms depending on the severity of the case.

Mild hypoglycemia can lead to feelings of nausea and hunger. The patient may also feel nervous, jittery and have fast heart beats. Sweaty skin, clammy and cold skin are likely symptoms.

Moderate hypoglycemia can result in a short temper, confusion, nervousness, fear and blurring of vision. The patient may feel weak and unsteady.

Severe cases of hypoglycemia can lead to seizures, coma, fainting spells, nightmares, headaches, excessive sweats and severe tiredness.

Diagnosis of low blood sugar

A doctor can diagnosis this medical condition by asking the patient questions and testing blood and urine samples. Home testing kits are available for patients to monitor blood sugar levels. It is important to see a qualified doctor though. The doctor can administer tests to ensure that will safely rule out other medical conditions that could affect blood sugar levels.

Treatment

Quick treatments include drinking or eating foods and drinks with high sugar contents. Good examples include soda, fruit juice, hard candy and raisins. Glucose energy tablets can also help. Doctors may also recommend medications and well as changes in diet and exercise routine to treat chronic low blood sugar.

9. Based on the article, which of the following is true?

    a. Low blood sugar can happen to anyone.

    b. Low blood sugar only happens to diabetics.

    c. Low blood sugar can occur even.

    d. None of the statements are true.

10. Which of the following are the author's opinion?

    a. Quick treatments include drinking or eating foods and drinks with high sugar contents.

    b. None of the statements are opinions.

    c. This condition can occur in diabetics and also in healthy adults.

    d. There are different symptoms depending on the severity of the case

11. What is the author's purpose?

a. To inform
b. To persuade
c. To entertain
d. To analyze

12. Which of the following is not a detail?

a. A doctor can diagnosis this medical condition by asking the patient questions and testing.
b. A doctor will test blood and urine samples.
c. Glucose energy tablets can also help.
d. Home test kits monitor blood sugar levels.

Chapter 1 - Getting Started

A Better Score Is Possible 6
Types of Multiple Choice 9
Multiple Choice Step-by-Step 12
Tips for Reading the Instructions 13
General Multiple Choice Tips 14
Multiple Choice Strategy Practice 20
Answer Key 39

13. Based on the partial Table of Contents above, what is this book about?

a. How to answer multiple choice questions
b. Different types of multiple choice questions
c. How to write a test
d. None of the above

Questions 14-17 refer to the following passage.

Myths, Legend and Folklore

Cultural historians draw a distinction between myth, legend and folktale simply as a way to group traditional stories. However, in many cultures, drawing a sharp line between myths and legends is not that simple. Instead of dividing their traditional stories into myths, legends, and folktales, some cultures divide them into two categories. The first category roughly corresponds to folktales, and the second is one that combines myths and legends. Similarly, we can not always separate myths from folktales. One society might consider a story true, making it a myth. Another society may believe the story is fiction, which makes it a folktale. In fact, when a myth loses its status as part of a religious system, it often takes on traits more typical of folktales, with its formerly divine characters now appearing as human heroes, giants, or fairies. Myth, legend, and folktale are only a few of the categories of traditional stories. Other categories include anecdotes and some kinds of jokes. Traditional stories, in turn, are only one category within the much larger category of folklore, which also includes items such as gestures, costumes, and music. [7]

14. The main idea of this passage is that

    a. Myths, fables, and folktales are not the same thing, and each describes a specific type of story

    b. Traditional stories can be categorized in different ways by different people

    c. Cultures use myths for religious purposes, and when this is no longer true, the people forget and discard these myths

    d. Myths can never become folk tales, because one is true, and the other is false

15. The terms myth and legend are

  a. Categories that are synonymous with true and false

  b. Categories that group traditional stories according to certain characteristics

  c. Interchangeable, because both terms mean a story that is passed down from generation to generation

  d. Meant to distinguish between a story that involves a hero and a cultural message and a story meant only to entertain

16. Traditional story categories not only include myths and legends, but

  a. Can also include gestures, since some cultures passed these down before the written and spoken word

  b. In addition, folklore refers to stories involving fables and fairy tales

  c. These story categories can also include folk music and traditional dress

  d. Traditional stories themselves are a part of the larger category of folklore, which may also include costumes, gestures, and music

17. This passage shows that

  a. There is a distinct difference between a myth and a legend, although both are folktales

  b. Myths are folktales, but folktales are not myths

  c. Myths, legends, and folktales play an important part in tradition and the past, and are a rich and colorful part of history

  d. Most cultures consider myths to be true

Questions 18 - 20 refer to the following passage.

Lowest Price Guarantee

Get it for less. Guaranteed!

ABC Electric will beat any advertised price by 10% of the difference.

> 1) If you find a lower advertised price, we will beat it by 10% of the difference.
>
> 2) If you find a lower advertised price within 30 days* of your purchase we will beat it by 10% of the difference.
>
> 3) If our own price is reduced within 30 days* of your purchase, bring in your receipt and we will refund the difference.

*14 days for computers, monitors, printers, laptops, tablets, cellular & wireless devices, home security products, projectors, camcorders, digital cameras, radar detectors, portable DVD players, DJ and pro-audio equipment, and air conditioners.

18. I bought a radar detector 15 days ago and saw an ad for the same model only cheaper. Can I get 10% of the difference refunded?

> a. Yes. Since it is less than 30 days, you can get 10% of the difference refunded.
>
> b. No. Since it is more than 14 days, you cannot get 10% of the difference re-funded.
>
> c. It depends on the cashier.
>
> d. Yes. You can get the difference refunded.

19. I bought a flat-screen TV for $500 10 days ago and found an advertisement for the same TV, at another store, on sale for $400. How much will ABC refund under this guarantee?

    a. $100
    b. $110
    c. $10
    d. $400

20. What is the purpose of this passage?

    a. To inform
    b. To educate
    c. To persuade
    d. To entertain

Questions 21 - 23 refer to the following passage.

Insects

Insects have segmented bodies supported by an exoskeleton, a hard outer covering made mostly of chitin. The segments of the body are organized into three distinctive connected units, a head, a thorax, and an abdomen. The head supports a pair of antennae, a pair of compound eyes, and three sets of appendages that form the mouthparts.

The thorax has six segmented legs and, if present in the species, two or four wings. The abdomen consists of eleven segments, though in a few species these segments may be fused together or very small.

Overall, there are 24 segments. The abdomen also contains most of the digestive, respiratory, excretory and reproductive internal structures. There is considerable variation and many adaptations in the body parts of insects especially wings, legs, antenna and mouthparts. [8]

21. How many units do insects have?

   a. Insects are divided into 24 units.

   b. Insects are divided into 3 units.

   c. Insects are divided into segments not units.

   d. It depends on the species.

22. Which of the following is true?

   a. All insects have 2 wings.

   b. All insects have 4 wings.

   c. Some insects have 2 wings.

   d. Some insects have 2 or 4 wings.

23. What is true of insect's abdomen?

   a. It contains some of the organs.

   b. It is too small for any organs.

   c. It contains all of the organs.

   d. None of the above.

Questions 24 - 27 refer to the following passage.

The Daffodils
by William Wordsworth

I wandered lonely as a cloud
That floats on high o'er vales and hills,
When all at once I saw a crowd,
A host, of golden daffodils;
Beside the lake, beneath the trees,
Fluttering and dancing in the breeze.

Continuous as the stars that shine
And twinkle on the Milky Way,
They stretched in never-ending line
Along the margin of a bay:

Ten thousand saw I at a glance,
Tossing their heads in sprightly dance.

The waves beside them danced, but they
Out-did the sparkling waves in glee:
A Poet could not but be gay,
In such a jocund company:
I gazed--and gazed--but little thought
What wealth the show to me had brought:

For oft, when on my couch I lie
In vacant or in pensive mood,
They flash upon that inward eye
Which is the bliss of solitude;
And then my heart with pleasure fills,
And dances with the daffodils.

24. Is the author of this poem a lover of nature?

    a. Yes

    b. No

    c. Uncertain. There isn't enough information

25. What is the general mood of this poem?

    a. Sad

    b. Thoughtful

    c. Happy

    d. Excited

26. What does sprightly mean?

    a. Growing very fast

    b. Sad and melancholy

    c. Weak and slow

    d. Happy and full of life

27. What is jocund company?

   a. Sad
   b. Happy
   c. Joyful
   d. Boring

Questions 28 - 30 refer to the following passage.

Blood

Blood is a specialized bodily fluid that delivers nutrients and oxygen to the body's cells and transports waste products away.

In vertebrates, blood consists of blood cells suspended in a liquid called blood plasma. Plasma, which comprises 55% of blood fluid, is mostly water (90% by volume), and contains dissolved proteins, glucose, mineral ions, hormones, carbon dioxide, platelets and the blood cells themselves.

Blood cells are mainly red blood cells (also called RBCs or erythrocytes) and white blood cells, including leukocytes and platelets. Red blood cells are the most abundant cells, and contain an iron-containing protein called hemoglobin that transports oxygen through the body.

The pumping action of the heart circulates blood around the body through blood vessels. In animals with lungs, arterial blood carries oxygen from inhaled air to the tissues of the body, and venous blood carries carbon dioxide, a waste product of metabolism produced by cells, from the tissues to the lungs to be exhaled. [9]

Practice Test Questions 2

28. What can we infer from the first paragraph in this passage?

    a. Blood is responsible for transporting oxygen to the cells.

    b. Blood is only red when it reaches the outside of the body.

    c. Each person has about six pints of blood.

    d. Blood's true function was only learned in the last century.

29. Which of these is not contained in blood plasma?

    a. Hormones

    b. Mineral ions

    c. Calcium

    d. Glucose

30. Which body part exhales carbon dioxide after venous blood has carried it from body tissues?

    a. The lungs

    b. The skin cells

    c. The bowels

    d. The sweat glands

Mathematics

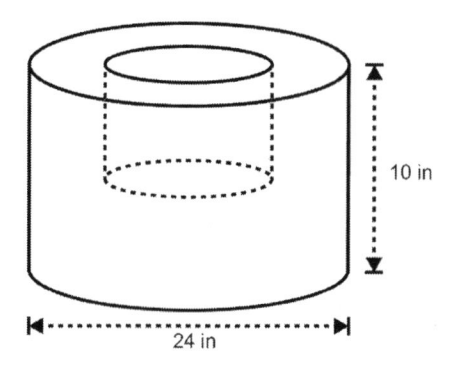

1. What is the volume of the above solid made by a hollow cylinder with half in size of the larger cylinder?

    a. 1440 π in³
    b. 1260 π in³
    c. 1040 π in³
    d. 960 π in³

2. Driver B drove his car 20 km/h faster than the driver A, and driver B travelled 480 km 2 hours before driver A. What was the speed of driver A?

    a. 70
    b. 80
    c. 60
    d. 90

3. If a train travels at 72 kilometers per hour, how far will it travel in 12 seconds?

    a. 200 meters
    b. 220 meters
    c. 240 meters
    d. 260 meters

4. Tony bought 15 dozen eggs for $80. 16 eggs were broken during loading and unloading. He sold the remaining eggs for $0.54 each. What will be his percent profit?

    a. 11%
    b. 11.2%
    c. 11.5%
    d. 12%

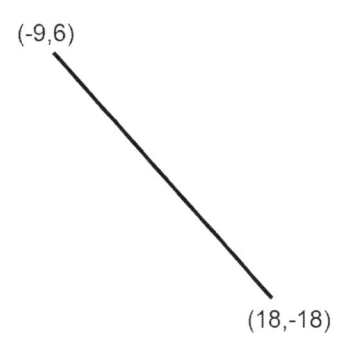

(-9,6)

(18,-18)

5. What is the slope of the line above?

    a. -8/9
    b. 9/8
    c. -9/8
    d. 8/9

6. Using the quadratic formula, solve the quadratic equation:

$$\frac{x+2}{x-2} + \frac{x-2}{x+2} = 0$$

    a. It has infinite numbers of solutions
    b. 0 and 1
    c. It has no solutions
    d. 0

7. Turn the following expression into a simple polynomial:

$5(3x^2 - 2) - x^2(2 - 3x)$

    a. $3x^3 + 17x^2 - 10$
    b. $3x^3 + 13x^2 + 10$
    c. $-3x^3 - 13x^2 - 10$
    d. $3x^3 + 13x^2 - 10$

8. In a class of 83 students, 72 are present. What percent of students are absent?

    a. 12%
    b. 13%
    c. 14%
    d. 15%

9. Solve $(x^3 + 2)(x^2 - x) - x^5$.

    a. $2x^5 - x^4 + 2x^2 - 2x$
    b. $-x^4 + 2x^2 - 2x$
    c. $-x^4 - 2x^2 - 2x$
    d. $-x^4 + 2x^2 + 2x$

10. 9ab² + 8ab² =

    a. ab^2
    b. $17ab^2$
    c. 17
    d. $17a^2b^2$

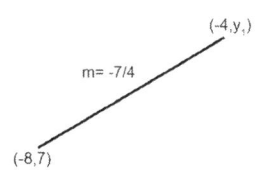

```
                    (-4,y₁)
        m= -7/4
  (-8,7)
```

11. With the data given above, what is the value of y_1?

    a. 0
    b. -7
    c. 7
    d. 8

12. Using the factoring method, solve the quadratic equation: $x^2 + 12x - 13 = 0$

    a. -13 and 1
    b. -13 and -1
    c. 1 and 13
    d. -1 and 13

13. In a local election at polling station A, 945 voters cast their vote out of 1270 registered voters. At polling station B, 860 cast their vote out of 1050 registered voters and at station C, 1210 cast their vote out of 1440 registered voters. What was the total turnout including all three polling stations?

    a. 70%
    b. 74%
    c. 76%
    d. 80%

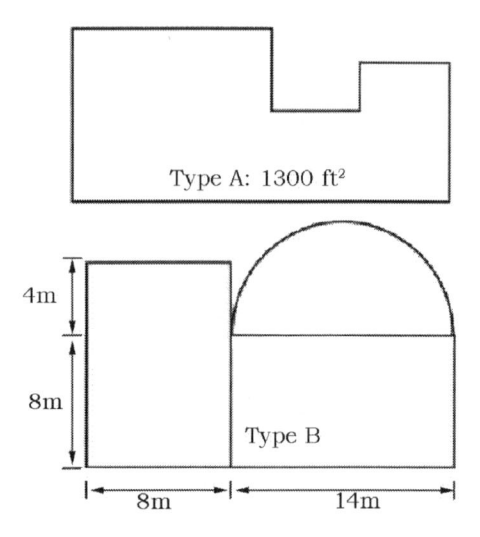

Type A: 1300 ft²

4m

8m

Type B

8m   14m

14. The price of houses in a certain subdivision is based on the total area. Susan is watching her budget and wants to choose the house with the lowest area. Which house type, A (1300 ft²) or B, should she choose if she would like the house with the lowest price?
(1cm² = 4.0ft² & π = 22/7)

    a. Type B is smaller 140 ft²
    b. Type A is smaller
    c. Type B is smaller at 855 ft²

d. Type B is larger

15. Find the mean of these set of numbers: 1, 2, 3, 4, 5, 6, 7, 8, 9, 10.

    a. 55
    b. 5.5
    c. 11
    d. 10

16. If a and b are real numbers, solve the following equation: (a + 2)x - b = -2 + (a + b)x

    a. -1
    b. 0
    c. 1
    d. 2

17. The area of a rectangle is 20 cm^2. If one side increases by 1 cm and other by 2 cm, the area of the new rectangle is 35 cm^2. Find the sides of the original rectangle.

    a. (4,8)
    b. (4,5)
    c. (2.5,8)
    d. b and c

18. Below are the number of people that attended a particular church every Friday for 7 weeks. Find the mean. 62, 18, 39, 13, 16, 37, 25.

    a. 25
    b. 210
    c. 62
    d. 30

19. Consider the following graph.

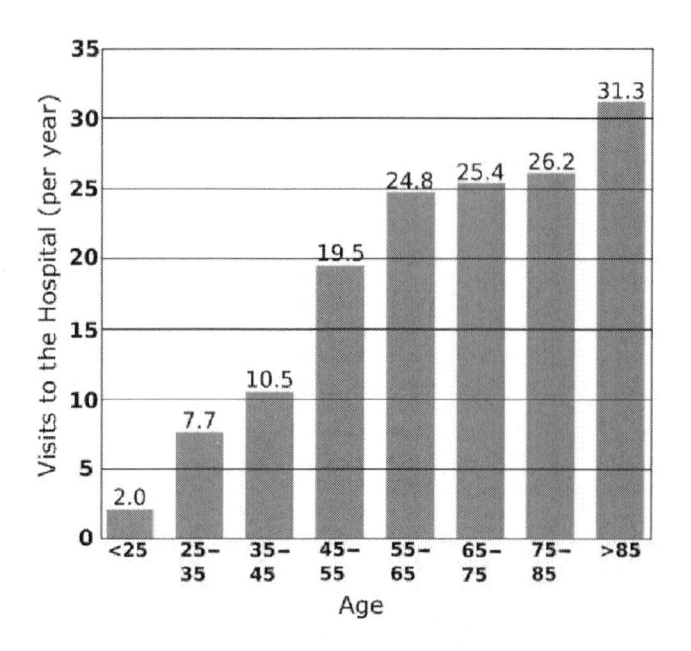

How many hospital visits per year does a person aged 85 or more make?

    a. 26.2

    b. 31.3

    c. More than 31.3

    d. A decision cannot be made from this graph.

20. Based on this graph, how many visits per year do you expect a person that is 95 or older to make?

    a. More than 31.3

    b. Less than 31.3

    c. 31.3

    d. A decision cannot be made from this graph.

21. How much water can be stored in a cylindrical container 5 meters in diameter and 12 meters high?

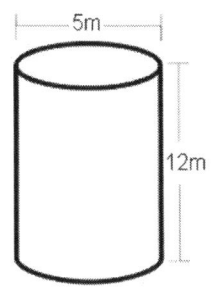

|―――5m―――|

12m

 a. 235.65 m³
 b. 223.65 m³
 c. 240.65 m³
 d. 252.65 m³

22. Find the solution for the following linear equation: 1/4 x - 2 = 5/6

 a. 0.2
 b. 0.4
 c. 0.6
 d. 0.8

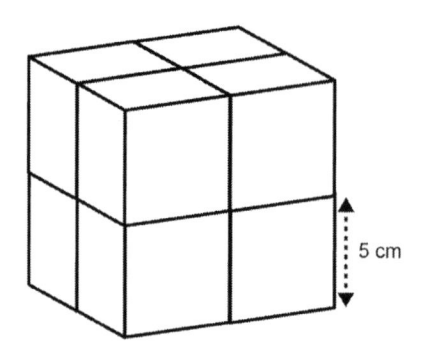

23. What is the volume of the figure above?

    a. 125 cm³
    b. 875 cm³
    c. 1000 cm³
    d. 500 cm³

24. Choose the expression the figure represents.

    a. X > 2
    b. X ≥ 2
    c. X < 2
    d. X ≤ 2

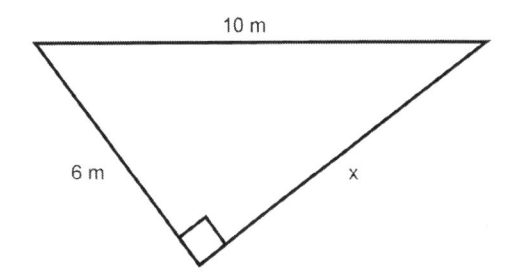

25. What is the length of the missing side in the triangle above?

    a. 6
    b. 4
    c. 8
    d. 5

26. Solve
$x \sqrt{5} - y = \sqrt{5}$
$x - y \sqrt{5} = 5$

    a. $(0, -\sqrt{5})$
    b. $(0, \sqrt{5})$
    c. $(-\sqrt{5}, 0)$
    d. $(\sqrt{5}, 0)$

27. If $A = -2x^4 + x^2 - 3x$, $B = x^4 - x^3 + 5$ and $C = x^4 + 2x^3 + 4x + 5$, find $A + B - C$.

    a. $x^3 + x^2 + x + 10$
    b. $-3x^3 + x^2 - 7x + 10$
    c. $-2x^4 - 3x^3 + x^2 - 7x$
    d. $-3x^4 + x^3 + x^2 - 7x$

28. Find the median of this set of numbers: 1,2,3,4,5,6,7,8,9 and 10

    a. 55
    b. 10
    c. 1
    d. 5.5

29. Convert 0.00002011 to scientific notation

    a. 2.011×10^{-4}
    b. 2.011×10^{5}
    c. 2.011×10^{-6}
    d. 2.011×10^{-5}

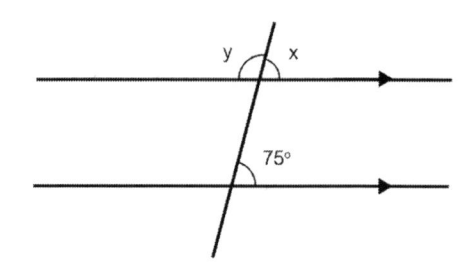

30. What is the value of the angle y?

    a. 25°
    b. 15°
    c. 30°
    d. 105°

31. Find the square of 25/9

    a. 5/3
    b. 3/5
    c. 7 58/81
    d. 15/2

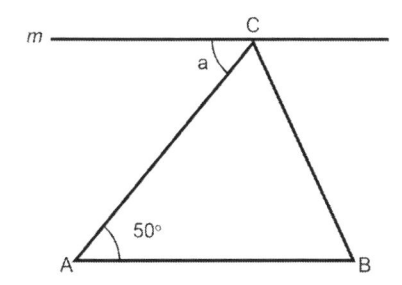

32. If the line *m* is parallel to the side AB of △ABC, what is angle *a*?

    a. 130°
    b. 25°
    c. 65°
    d. 50°

33. Find the median of this set of numbers: 100, 200, 450, 29, 1029, 300 and 2001

    a. 300
    b. 29
    c. 7
    d. 4,080

34. Which one of the following is less than a third?

    a. 84/231
    b. 6/35
    c. 3/22
    d. b and c

35. Which of the following numbers is the largest?

   a. 1
   b. $\sqrt{2}$
   c. 3/2
   d. 4/3

36. $(4Y^3 - 2Y^2) + (7Y^2 + 3y - y) =$

   a. $4y^3 + 9y^2 + 4y$
   b. $5y^3 + 5y^2 + 3y$
   c. $4y^3 + 7y^2 + 2y$
   d. $4y^3 + 5y^2 + 2y$

37. $7(2y + 8) + 1 - 4(y + 5) =$

   a. 10y + 36
   b. 10y + 77
   c. 18y + 37
   d. 10y + 37

(18,12)

(9,-6)

38. What is the distance between the two points?

   a. ≈19
   b. 20
   c. ≈21
   d. ≈20

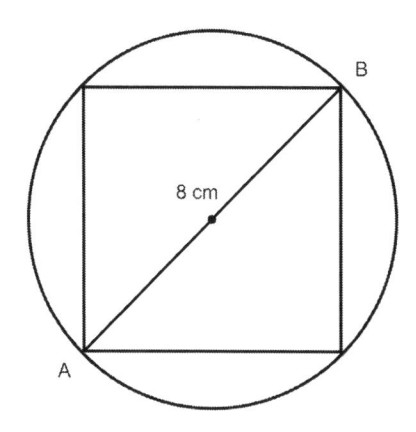

39. What is area of the circle?

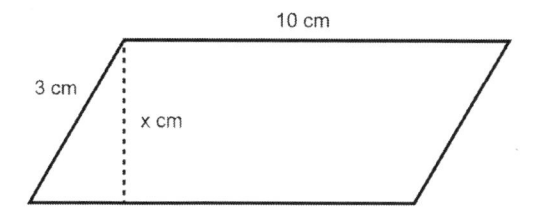

    a. 4 π cm²
    b. 12 π cm²
    c. 10 π cm²
    d. 16 π cm²

40. What is the perimeter of the parallelogram above?

    a. 12 cm
    b. 26 cm
    c. 13 cm
    d. (13+x) cm

41. Richard gives 's' amount of salary to each of his 'n' employees weekly. If he has 'x' amount of money then how many days he can employ these 'n' employees.

a. sx/7n
b. 7x/nx
c. nx/7s
d. 7x/ns

42. Find the mode from these test results: 17, 19, 18, 17, 18, 19, 11, 17, 16, 19, 15, 15, 15, 17, 13, 11

a. 15
b. 11
c. 17
d. 19

43. A map uses a scale of 1:100,000. How much distance on the ground is 3 inches on the map if the scale is in inches?

a. 13 inches
b. 300,000 inches
c. 30,000 inches
d. 333.999 inches

44. Subtract 456,890 from 465,890.

a. 9,000
b. 7000
c. 8970
d. 8500

45. Susan wants to buy a leather jacket that costs $545.00 and is on sale for 10% off. What is the approximate cost?

    a. $525
    b. $450
    c. $475
    d. $500

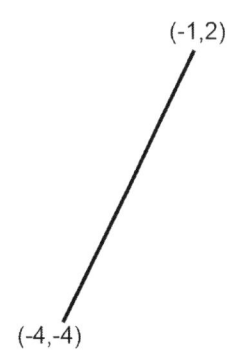

(-1,2)

(-4,-4)

46. What is the slope of the line above?

    a. 1
    b. 2
    c. 3
    d. -2

47. Convert 204 to scientific notation.

    a. 2.04×10^{-2}
    b. 0.204×10^{2}
    c. 2.04×10^{3}
    d. 2.04×10^{2}

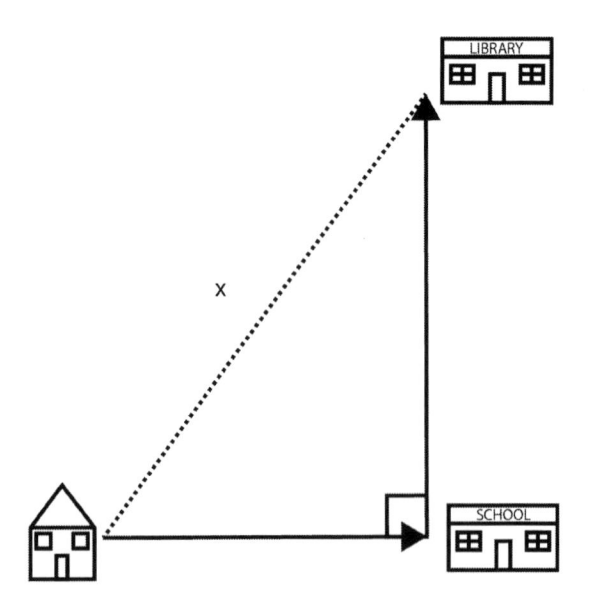

48. Every day starting from his home Peter travels due east 3 kilometers to the school. After school he travels due north 4 kilometers to the library. What is the distance between Peter's home and the library?

    a. 15 km
    b. 10 km
    c. 5 km
    d. 12 ½ km

Bar Graph Data

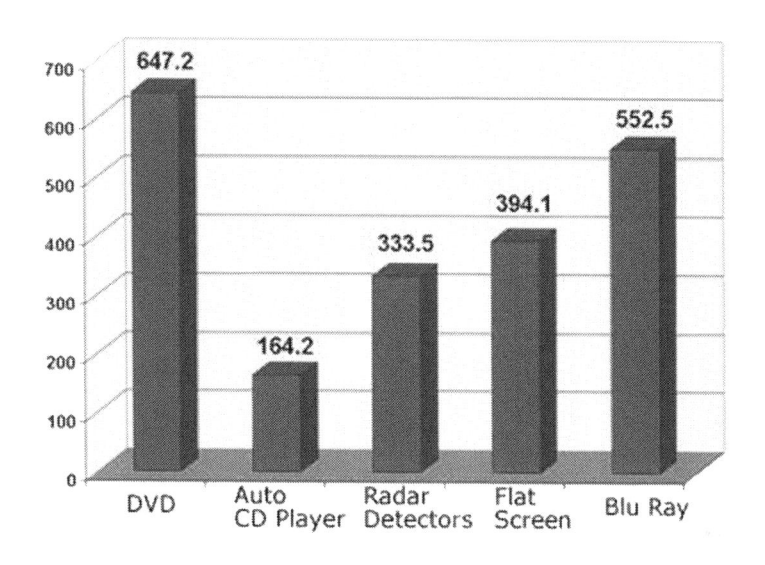

- DVD: 647.2
- Auto CD Player: 164.2
- Radar Detectors: 333.5
- Flat Screen: 394.1
- Blu Ray: 552.5

49. Consider the graph above. What is the third best-selling product?

    a. Radar Detectors

    b. Flat Screen

    c. Blu Ray

    d. Auto CD Players

50. Which two products are the closest in the number of sales?

    a. Blu Ray and Flat Screen TV

    b. Flat Screen TV and Radar Detectors

    c. Radar Detectors and Auto CD Players

    d. DVD players and Blu Ray

English Grammar and Usage

1. Elaine promised to bring the camera _____ at the mall yesterday.

    a. by me
    b. with me
    c. at me
    d. to me

2. Last night, he _____ the sleeping bag down beside my mattress.

    a. lay
    b. laid
    c. lain
    d. has laid

3. I would have bought the shirt for you if

    a. I had known you liked it.
    b. I have known you liked it.
    c. I would know you liked it.
    d. I know you liked it.

4. Many believers still hope _____ proof of the existence of ghosts.

    a. two find
    b. to find
    c. to found
    d. to have been found

5. Choose the sentence with the correct grammar.

    a. The court summons was placed on his desk

    b. The court summons are placed on his desk

    c. The court summons were placed on his desk

    d. None of the above

6. If he _____ the textbook like he was supposed to, he would have known what was on the test.

    a. will have read

    b. shouldn't have read

    c. would have read

    d. had read

7. Following the tornado, telephone poles _____ all over the street.

    a. laid

    b. lied

    c. were lying

    d. were laying

8. Choose the sentence with the correct grammar.

    a. Neither the teacher nor the students is left in class.

    b. Neither the teacher nor the students was left in class.

    c. Neither the teacher nor the students are left in class.

    d. None of the above.

9. After the car was fixed, it _____ again.

    a. ran good

    b. ran well

    c. would have run well

    d. ran more well

10. Choose the correct sentence.

   a. Their only employee with a nose ring is a young man named Daniel.

   b. Their only employee is a young man named Daniel with a nose ring.

   c. Their only employee is a young man with a nose ring named Daniel.

   d. A and C are correct.

11. Choose the sentence with the correct grammar.

   a. Everyone are to wear a black tie.

   b. Everyone have to wear a black tie.

   c. Everyone has to wear a black tie.

   d. None of the above.

12. Choose the sentence with the correct grammar.

   a. The salmon has been cooked.

   b. The salmon have been cooked.

   c. Both of the above.

   d. None of the above.

13. The Ford Motor Company was named for Henry Ford, _____.

   a. which had founded the company.

   b. who founded the company.

   c. whose had founded the company.

   d. whom had founded the company.

14. The weatherman on Channel 6 said that this has been the _____.

    a. most hotter summer on record

    b. most hottest summer on record

    c. hottest summer on record

    d. hotter summer on record

15. As the tallest monument in the United States, the St. Louis Arch _____.

    a. has rose to an impressive 630 feet.

    b. is risen to an impressive 630 feet.

    c. rises to an impressive 630 feet.

    d. was rose to an impressive 630 feet.

Essay Revision

Abuse of Science: The Atom Bomb

The cost of the two World Wars – not to mention the lives lost – could have easily paid for the entire energy consumption of the nations which waged them. [1] Even today, world powers are spending hundreds of billions of dollars sponsoring wars in a bid to control oil-rich areas. [2] Spending such astronomic sums on peaceful, environment friendly sources of energy would certainly produce results that would limit the energy needs of the planet as a whole. [3] Not to mention, resolving the conflicts between warring nations. [4]

For instance the atom bomb was developed during the Second World War by the recommendations of the great Albert Einstein - who is accepted as the father of modern physics; in fear of the Germans developing it and using on the Allies. [5] The technology behind the atom bomb essentially had the power to resolve the war, which scientists like him failed to convey. [6] Using it to produce energy for power was an option wide open to be explored by scientists. [7] Today, as many as forty countries including countries like Egypt, harness nuclear energy as a dominant source of power alongside mainstream carbon sources. [8]

The two atom bombs dropped at Hiroshima and Nagasaki, as the consequence of the tragedy at Pearl Harbor, left catastrophic legacies to the generations that followed. [9] The generations that followed still have not recovered from the genetic disorders. [10] Almost seven decades passing later, abnormal births and birth defects continue to occur. [11]

1. Which sentence from the passage is an example of a sentence fragment?

    a. 3
    b. 4
    c. 5
    d. 6

2. Which of the following changes would focus attention on the main idea of the second paragraph?

    a. Yet, the technology behind the atom bomb essentially had the power of resolving the war itself which scientists like him failed to convey.

    b. As a result of that, the technology behind the atom bomb essentially had the power of resolving the war itself which scientists like him failed to convey.

    c. With respect to that, the technology behind the atom bomb essentially had the power of resolving the war itself which scientists like him failed to convey.

    d. Additionally, the technology behind the atom bomb essentially had the power of resolving the war itself which scientists like him failed to convey.

Practice Test Questions 2   119

3. Which of the following are needed in sentence 5?

a. For instance the atom bomb was developed during the Second World War by the recommendations of the great Albert Einstein - who is accepted as the father of modern physics - in fear of the Germans developing it and using on the Allies.

b. For instance, the atom bomb was developed during the Second World War by the recommendations of the great Albert Einstein - who is accepted as the father of modern physics - in fear of the Germans developing it and using on the Allies.

c. For instance, the atom bomb was developed during the Second World War by the recommendations of the great Albert Einstein; who is accepted as the father of modern physics - in fear of the Germans developing it and using on the Allies.

d. For instance, the atom bomb was developed during the Second World War by the recommendations of the great Albert Einstein; who is accepted as the father of modern physics, in fear of the Germans developing it and using on the Allies.

4. Which of the following sentences, if inserted before sentence 7, would best illustrate the main idea of the passage?

a. The name of the technology is widely referred to in current science books published worldwide as nuclear fission.

b. This technology is, however, misused by many irresponsible states in the world today.

c. Nuclear fission that is used in the fuelling of the bomb, has the capacity to produce electrical energy which has turned out to be a major alternative later in the Twentieth Century.

d. Nuclear fission, which is the main technology behind the development of the atom bomb can also be used to produce gamma rays which has many applications in medical science.

Leg Surgery

The main reason many young women opt for surgery despite the pain, inconvenience and cost, is the height discrimination in an increasingly competitive job market. [1] Almost all firms put certain height criteria for the candidates who apply. [2] For example, for an air stewardess position, women must be no more than 163 cm tall; whereas for jobs in foreign affairs, Chinese diplomats are required to match their foreign counterparts. [3] Height concerns also effect routine citizenship privileges such as driving licenses, which require a height of at least 157 cm to be eligible for taking the test in some places. [4]

The urge to undergo surgery is becoming increasingly popular among Chinese males as well. [5] "It offers me a 10 cm increase in my height, which can dramatically change my future," says Jing Yong, an interpreter working in Hong Kong. [6] "This will allow me better opportunities in the competitive job market here," adds the young multilingual who couldn't make it to the foreign ministry for being below 168 cm. [7] Even parents approve of the idea, being fully aware of all the complexity and they are willing to finance such a labyrinth surgery. [8] "It's something that will give her confidence and achieve her goals in life. [9] Her height used to bother her tremendously, now this can change that," comments Swee Jing's father by her bedside as she is recovering from the eighteen-months process that involves elongating her tibia and fibula by placing two rods that will stimulate the extra growth of the bones. [10] They too are hopeful about the possibilities the surgery would affect the life of their daughter. [11]

5. Which sentence in the second paragraph is least relevant to the main idea of the first paragraph?

    a. 2
    b. 3
    c. 4
    d. 5

6. Which sentence is not consistent with the author's purpose?

    a. 3
    b. 6
    c. 9
    d. 12

7. Which of the following sentences, if inserted after sentence 7, would best illustrate the main idea of the passage?

    a. This is the main reason I am willing to undergo this surgery

    b. This artificial way of gaining height is turning out to be a new trend among the new generation in height conscious China.

    c. Height is a very big problem for Chinese people, particularly for those who wish to go abroad and carry the flag of China there.

    d. Young people like Yong will have to spend the rest of their lives with a fake pair of legs though.

8. Which of the following changes are needed in sentence 8?

    a. Even parents approve of the idea, being fully aware of all the sophistications and they are willing to finance such a labyrinth surgery.

    b. Even parents approve of the idea, being fully aware of all the complications and they are willing to finance such a sophisticated surgery.

    c. Even parents approve of the idea, being fully aware of all the complexity and they are willing to finance such a sophisticated surgery.

    d. Even parents approve of the idea, being fully aware of all the complexity and they are willing to finance such a sophisticated surgery.

My Friend Luke

My forty-year old friend Luke is possibly the sweetest, shyest person enjoying his life on the entire Earth. [1] He is somewhat short, skinny and upright; has a thin moustache and a thinner trace of hair covering his head. [2] And since he has problems seeing distant things, he wears glasses that are small, thick and frameless; the round coffee-brown colored glasses give him a cool appearance uniquely suited to his personality. [3] Which I doubt belongs to any other person. [4]

There are traits in him seldom found in others. [5] While in the crowd, he walks sideways so as not to trouble others. [6] Instead of requesting a space to move ahead, he glides past to one side of the person blocking in his way. [7] If the gap turns out to be so narrow that it does not permit his bony frame to pass, he waits patiently for the person to move out of the way. [8] He is panicked by street dogs and neighbors' cats and to avoid them, he crosses to the other side of the street every now and then. [9]

Luke never speaks, as he thinks speaking is actually a waste of energy; something he is vehemently dedicated to saving. [10] Whenever he does, in order not to interrupt anybody, he speaks with a very soft, low tone – in a way no one ever notices him speaking in the first place. [11] Quite ironically, when he gets a rare chance to speak, he never succeeds in speaking more than two words before getting interrupted by others. [12]

9. What sentence from the passage is an example of a sentence fragment?

    a. 4
    b. 5
    c. 6
    d. 7

10. Which sentence in the second paragraph is least relevant to the main idea of the second paragraph?

    a. 6
    b. 7
    c. 8
    d. 9

11. Which of the following sentences should be modified to reduce redundancy?

    a. 2
    b. 3
    c. 4
    d. 5

12. Which of the following sentences, if inserted before sentence 1, would best illustrate the main idea of the passage?

    a. But that does not bother him; rather he always seems to be happy in being able to utter those two words.

    b. Interestingly, he never insists in speaking with people more eloquently.

    c. What is more ironic, he never worked on his social skills and diction to be more communicative.

    d. As a result, Luke feels like hitting those interrupting him in their face.

Answer Key

Reading Comprehension

1. B
We can infer an important part of the respiratory system are the lungs. From the passage, "Molecules of oxygen and carbon dioxide are passively exchanged, by diffusion, between the gaseous external environment and the blood. This exchange process occurs in the alveolar region of the lungs." Therefore, one of the primary functions for the respiratory system is the exchange of oxygen and carbon dioxide, and this process occurs in the lungs. We can therefore infer that the lungs are an important part of the respiratory system.

2. C
The process by which molecules of oxygen and carbon dioxide are passively exchanged is diffusion.
This is a definition type question. Scan the passage for references to "oxygen," "carbon dioxide," or "exchanged."

3. A
The organ that plays an important role in gas exchange in amphibians is the skin.
Scan the passage for references to "amphibians," and find the answer.

4. A
The three physiological zones of the respiratory system are Conducting, transitional, respiratory zones.

5. B
This warranty does not cover a product that you have tried to fix yourself. From paragraph two, "This limited warranty does not cover ... any unauthorized disassembly, repair, or modification. "

6. C
ABC Electric could either replace or repair the fan, provided the other conditions are met. ABC Electric has the option to

repair or replace.

7. B
The warranty does not cover a stove damaged in a flood. From the passage, "This limited warranty does not cover any damage to the product from improper installation, accident, abuse, misuse, natural disaster, insufficient or excessive electrical supply, abnormal mechanical or environmental conditions."

A flood is an "abnormal environmental condition," and a natural disaster, so it is not covered.

8. A
A missing part is an example of defective workmanship. This is an error made in the manufacturing process. A defective part is not considered workmanship.

9. A
Low blood sugar occurs both in diabetics and healthy adults.

10. B
None of the statements are the author's opinion.

11. A
The author's purpose is the inform.

12. A
The only statement that is not a detail is, "A doctor can diagnosis this medical condition by asking the patient questions and testing."

13. A
Based on the partial table of contents, this book is most likely about how to answer multiple choice.

14. B
This passage describes the different categories for traditional stories. The other options are facts from the passage, not the main idea of the passage. The main idea of a passage will always be the most general statement. For example, Option A, Myths, fables, and folktales are not the same thing, and each describes a specific type of story. This is a true state-

ment from the passage, but not the main idea of the passage, since the passage also talks about how some cultures may classify a story as a myth and others as a folktale. The statement, from Option B, Traditional stories can be categorized in different ways by different people, is a more general statement that describes the passage.

15. B
Option B is the best choice, categories that group traditional stories according to certain characteristics.

Options A and C are false and can be eliminated right away. Option D is designed to confuse. Option D may be true, but it is not mentioned in the passage.

16. D
The best answer is D, traditional stories themselves are a part of the larger category of folklore, which may also include costumes, gestures, and music.

All of the other options are false. Traditional stories are part of the larger category of Folklore, which includes other things, not the other way around.

17. A
There is a distinct difference between a myth and a legend, although both are folktales.

18. B
The time limit for radar detectors is 14 days. Since you made the purchase 15 days ago, you do not qualify for the guarantee.

19. B
Since you made the purchase 10 days ago, you are covered by the guarantee. Since it is an advertised price at a different store, ABC Electric will "beat" the price by 10% of the difference, which is,

500 – 400 = 100 – difference in price

100 X 10% = $10 – 10% of the difference

The advertised lower price is $400. ABC will beat this price by 10% so they will refund $100 + 10 = $110.

20. C
The purpose of this passage is to persuade.

21. B
From the first paragraph, "The segments of the body are organized into three distinctive connected units, a head, a thorax, and an abdomen."

This question tries to confuse 'segments' and 'units.'

22. D
This question tries to confuse. Read the passage carefully to find reference to the number of wings. "...if present in the species, two or four wings."
From this, we can conclude some insects have no wings, (if present ...) some have 2 wings and some have 4 wings.

23. A
The question asks about the abdomen and choices refer to organs in the abdomen. The passage says, "The abdomen also contains most of the digestive, respiratory, ... "

The choices are,

- a. It contains some of the organs.
- b. It is too small for any organs.
- c. It contains all of the organs.
- d. None of the above.

Choice A is true, but we need to see if there is better choice before answering. Choice B is not true. Choice C is not true since the relevant sentence says 'most' not 'all.' Choice D can be eliminated since Choice A is true.

Given there is not better choice, Choice A is the best choice answer.

24. A
The author is enjoying the daffodils very much and so we can infer that he is a lover of nature.

25. C
The mood of this poem is happy. From the last line,

And then my heart with pleasure fills,
And dances with the daffodils.

26. D
Sprightly means happy and full of life. From the lines before and after sprightly, we can see it means happy.

Ten thousand saw I at a glance,
Tossing their heads in sprightly dance.

The waves beside them danced, but they
Out-did the sparkling waves in glee:

27. C
Joyful is the best answer. Happy is a possible answer, but joyful is better. Jocund means jovial, exuberant, light-hearted; merry and in high spirits. From the poem,

Ten thousand saw I at a glance,
Tossing their heads in sprightly dance.

The waves beside them danced, but they
Out-did the sparkling waves in glee:

28. A
We can infer that blood is responsible for transporting oxygen to the cells.

29. C
Calcium is not contained in blood plasma.

From the passage, "[Blood Plasma] contains dissolved proteins, glucose, mineral ions, hormones, carbon dioxide, platelets and the blood cells themselves."

30. A
The lungs exhale the carbon dioxide after venous blood has been carried from body tissues.

Mathematics

1. B
Volume= Volume of large cylinder - Volume of small cylinder
(Volume of cylinder = area of base x height)
Volume= ($\pi\ 12^2$x 10) - ($\pi\ 6^2$x 5), $1440\pi - 180\pi$
Volume= $1260\pi\ in^3$

2. B
$V_b = V_a - 20$
$S = 480$
$t_a + 2 = t_b$

$S = V_a t_a$
$t_a = S/V_a$

$S = V_b t_b$
$480 = (V_a - 20)(t_a + 2)$
$480 = (V_a - 20)(480/V_a + 2)$
$480 = 480 + 2V_a - 2 - 480/V_a - 40$
$2V_a^2 - 40V_a - 9600 = 0$
$V_a^2 - 20V_a - 4800 = 0$

$V_{a1,2} = 20 \pm \sqrt{400 + 4 - 4800} / 2$
$V_{a1,2} = 20 \pm 140 / 2$

$V_a = 80$

3. C
1 hour is equal to 3600 seconds and 1 kilometer is equal to 1000 meters. So a train covers 72,000 meters in 36,000 seconds.
Distance covered in 12 seconds = 12 × 72,000/3,600 = 240 meters.

4. A
Remaining number of eggs that Tony sold = 12×15 − 16 = 164. Total amount for selling 164 eggs = 164×0.54 = $89.1.
Percentage profit = (89.1 − 80) × 100/80 = 11.25%
The answer is required with 2 significant digits, round off to 11%.

5. A
Slope (m) = change in y / change in x

$(x_1, y_1)=(-9,6)$ & $(x_2, y_2)= (18,-18)$
Slope = $(-18 – 6)/[18-(-9)]$ = $-24/27$ = $-8/9$

6. C
This equation has no solution.

$x^2 + 4x + 4 + x^2 - 4x + 4 / (x-2)(x + 2) = 0$

$2x^2 + 8 / (x-2)(x + 2) = 0 \Rightarrow 2x^2 + 8 = 0$

$x^2 + 4 = 0$

$x_{1,2} = 0 \pm \sqrt{-4 * 4} / 2$

$x_{1,2} = 0 \pm \sqrt{-16} / 2$

Solution for the square root of -16 is not a real number, so this equation has no solution.

7. D
$3x^3 + 13x^2 - 10$
$5(3x^2 - 2) - x^2(2 - 3x)$
$15x^2 - 10 - 2x^2 + 3x^3$
$3x^3 + 13x^2 - 10$

8. B
Absent students = 83 – 72 = 11
Percent of absent students = 11/83 X 100 = 13.25
Reducing up to two significant digits = 13%.

9. B
$-x^4 + 2x^2 - 2x$
$(x^3 + 2)(x^2 - x) - x^5$
$x^5 - x^4 + 2x^2 - 2x - x^5$
$-x^4 + 2x^2 - 2x$

10. B
$ab^2 (9 + 8) = 17ab^2$

Practice Test Questions 2   *131*

11. A
$x_1 = -4$, $(x_2, y_2) = (-8, 7)$ & slope $= -7/4$
$(7 - y_1)/[-8-(-4)] = -7/4$
$(7 - y_1)/-4 = -7/4$
$7 - y_1 = 7$
$y_1 = 0$

12. A
-13 and 1
$x^2 + 12x - 13$
$x^2 + 13x - x - 13 = 0$
$x(x + 13) - (x + 13) = 0$
$(x + 13)(x - 1) = 0$
$X = -13 \quad X = 1$

13. D
Total votes cast $= 945 + 860 + 1210 = 3015$
Total registered voters at all 3 polling stations $=$
$1270 + 1050 + 1440 = 3760$
Turnout $= 3015/3760 \times 100 = 80\%$

14. C
Area of Type B $= [(12 \times 8) + (14 \times 8) + (1/2 \times 22/7 \times 7^2)]$
$96 + 112 + 77$
$285 m^2$
Converting to feet $= 3 \times 285\ ft^2$
Area of Type B $= 855\ ft^2$

15. C
First add all the numbers $1 + 2 + 3 + 4 + 5 + 6 + 7 + 8 + 9 + 10 = 55$. Then divide by 10 (the number of data provided) $= 55/5 = 11$

16. A
$(a + 2)x - b = -2 + (a + b)x$
$ax + 2x - b = -2 + ax + bx$
$ax + 2x - ax - bx = -2 + b$
$2x - bx = -2 + b$
$(2 - b)x = -(2 - b)$
$x = -(2 - b) : (2 - b)$
$x = -1$

17. D
ab = 20 => a = 20/b
(a + 1) (b + 2) = 35

(20/b + 1) (b + 2) = 35
20 + 40/b + b + 2 = 35
20b + 40 + b² = 33b
b² - 13b + 40 = 0
$b_{1,2}$ = 13 ± √169 - 160 / 2
$b_{1,2}$ = 13 ± 3 / 2
b_1 = 8
b_2 = 5
a_1 = 20/b_1 = 20/8 = 2.5
a_2 = 20/b_2 = 20/5 = 4

18. D
First add all the numbers 62 + 18 + 39 + 13 + 16 + 37 + 25 = 210. Then divide by 7 (the number of data provided) = 210/7 = 30.

19. B
Based on this graph, a person that is 85 or older will make 31.3 visits to the hospital every year.

20. A
Based on this graph, the number of visits per year is going up as age goes up, so we can expect a person that is 95 to have more than 31.3 visits to the hospital each year.

21. B
The formula of the volume of cylinder is = ∏ r²h. Where ∏ is 3.142, r is radius of the cross sectional area, and h is the height. So the volume will be = 3.142×2.5² ×12 = 235.65 m³.

22. D
1/4x - 2 = 5/6
1 = 5 (4x - 2)/6
6 = 5(4x - 2)
6 = 20x - 10
-20x = -10 - -6
-20x = -16
x = -16/-20 = 0.8

23. C
Large cube is made up of 8 smaller cubes of 5 cm sides.
Volume = Volume of small cube x 8
Volume = (5 x 5 x 5) x 8, 125 x 8
Volume = 1000cm^3

24. A
The line is pointing towards numbers greater than 2. The equation is therefore, X < 2.

25. C
Pythagorean Theorem:
(Hypotenuse)^2 = (Perpendicular)^2 + (Base)^2
h^2 = a^2 + b^2

Given: a = 6, h = 10
h^2 = a^2 + b^2
b^2 = h^2 - a^2
b^2 = 10^2 + 6^2
b^2 = 100 – 36
b^2 = 64
b = 8

26. A
(0, -√5)

y = x√5 - √5
x - (x√5 - √5) √5 = 5
x - 5x + 5 = 5
-4x = 5 - 5
-4x = 0

y = x√5 - √5
y = 0√5 - √5
y = √5

27. C
-2x^4 - 3x^3 + x^2 - 7x
A + B - C = (-2x^4 + x^2 - 3x) + (x^4 - x^3 + 5) - (x^4 + 2x^3 + 4x + 5)
-2x^4 + x^2 - 3x + x^4 - x^3 + 5 - x^4 - 2x^3 - 4x - 5
-2x^4 - 3x^3 + x^2 - 7x

Remove the brackets, but change all signs in the third polynomial because of the minus sign. Now group the variables by degrees.

28. D
First arrange the numbers in a numerical sequence - 1,2,3,4,5,6,7,8,9, 10. Then find the middle number or numbers. The middle numbers are 5 and 6. The median = 5 + 6/2 = 11/2 = 5.5

29. D
The decimal point moves 5 places left to be placed after 2, which is the first non-zero number. Thus its 2.011×10^{-5}
The answer is in the negative because the decimal moved left

30. D
Two parallel lines intersected by a third line with angles of 75°
x = 75° (corresponding angles)
x + y = 180° (supplementary angles)
y = 180° - 75°
y = 105°

31. C
$(25/9)^2$ = 7 58/81

32. D
Two parallel lines(m & side AB) intersected by side AC
a = 50° (interior angles).

33. A
First arrange the numbers in a numerical sequence - 29,100, 200, 300, 450, 1029, 2001. Next find the middle number. The median = 300.

34. C
84/231 = 12/33 > 1/3
6/35 = 1/5 < 1/3
3/22 = 1/7 < 1/3

35. B
$\sqrt{2}$ is the largest number.
Here are the choices:

a. 1
b. $\sqrt{2}$ = 1.414
c. 3/22 = .1563
d. 4/3 = 1.33

36. D
Remove parenthesis
$4Y^3 - 2Y^2 + 7Y^2 + 3Y - Y =$
add and subtract like terms, $4Y^3 + 5Y^2 + 2Y$

37. D
Open parenthesis, (7 x 2y + 7 x 8) + 1- (4 x y -20) =
14y + 56 + 1 - 4y - 20,
Collect like terms =14y -4y + 56 + 1 – 20 = 10y + 37

38. D
Distance between 2 points = $[(x_2 - x_1)^2 + (y_2 - y_1)^2]^{1/2}$

Distance= $[(18-9)^2+(12+6)^2]^{1/2}$
Distance= $[(9)^2+(18)^2]^{1/2}$
Distance= $(81+324)^{1/2}$
Distance= $(405)^{1/2}$
Since 20^2 = 400 & 21^2 = 441, 19^2 = 361 therefore the distance is approx. 20.

39. D
Circle with given diameter and a square within the circle
Area of circle = π x r^2
Area of circle = π x 4^2
Area of circle = 16 π cm^2

40. B
Perimeter of a parallelogram is the sum of the sides.

Perimeter = 2(l + b)
Perimeter = 2(3 + 10), 2 x 13
Perimeter = 26 cm.

41. D
He pays 'ns' amount to the employees for 7 days. The 'x' amount will be for '7x/ns' days.

42. A
Simply find the most recurring number. The most occurring number in the series is 15.

43. B
1 inch on map = 100,000 inches on ground. So 3 inches on map = 3 x 100,000 = 300,000 inches on ground.

44. A
465,890 - 456,890 = 9,000.

45. D
The jacket costs $545.00 so we can round up to $550. 10% of $550 is 55. We can round down to $50, which is easier to work with. $550 - $50 is $500. The jacket will cost about $500.

The actual cost will be 10% X 545 = $54.50
545 – 54.50 = $490.50

46. B
Slope (m) = change in y
            change in x

$(x_1, y_1) = (-1, 2)$ & $(x_2, y_2) = (-4, -4)$
Slope = $(-4 – 2)/[-4 - (-1)]$ = $-6/-3$
Slope = 2

47. D
The decimal point moves 2 spaces right to be placed after 2, which is the first non-zero number. Thus it is 2.04×10^2

48. C
Pythagorean Theorem:
$(Hypotenuse)^2 = (Perpendicular)^2 + (Base)^2$
$h^2 = a^2 + b^2$

Pythagorean Theorem:
$(Hypotenuse)2 = (Perpendicular) 2 + (Base) 2$
$h^2 = a^2 + b^2$

Given: $3^2 + 4^2 = h^2$
h2 = 9 + 16

h = √25
h = 5

49. B
Flat Screen TVs are the third best-selling product.

50. B
The two products that are closest in the number of sales, are Flat Screen TVs and Radar Detectors.

English Grammar and Usage

1. D
The preposition "to" is correct. 'To' here means give.

2. A
"Lie" means to recline, and does not take an object. "lay" means to place and does take an object.

3. A
Past unreal conditional. Takes the form,
[If ... Past Perfect ..., ... would have + past participle ...]

4. B
This sentence is in the present tense, so "to find" is correct.

5. A
Always use the singular verb form for nouns like politics, wages, mathematics, innings, news, advice, summons, furniture, information, poetry, machinery, vacation, scenery etc.

6. D
When talking about something that didn't happen in the past, use the past perfect (if I had done).

7. C
"Lie" means to recline, and does not take an object. "Lay" means to place and does take an object. Peter lay the books on the table (the books are the direct object), or the telephone poles were lying on the road (no direct object).

8. C
If one of the subjects linked by "either," "or," "nor" or "neither" is in plural form, then the verb should also be in plural, and the verb should be close to the plural subject.

9. B
"Ran well" is correct. "Ran good" is never correct.

10. D
Both A and C are correct.

> a. Their only employee with a nose ring is a young man named Daniel.

> c. Their only employee is a young man with a nose ring named Daniel.

11. C
Use a singular verb with either, each, neither, everyone and many.

12. C
Nouns like deer, sheep, swine, salmon etc can take a singular or plural verb depending if they are used in their singular or plural form.

13. B
The sentence refers to a person, so "who" is the only correct option.

14. C
The superlative, "hottest," is used when expressing a temperature greater than that of anything to which it is being compared.

15. C
The simple present tense, "rises," is correct.

Essay Revision

1. B
Sentence 4 is a fragment. "Not to mention resolving the conflicts between warring nations."

This sentence is essentially a verbal phrase of the word "resolve" which does not have a main clause as part of the sentence. It is the extension of the sentence preceding it which contains the main clause and does make sense as it stands after the sentence with the main clause. However, since it does not have the main clause in its own structure, it is a sentence fragment.

2. A
The following changes would focus attention on the main idea in paragraph 2. "Yet, the technology behind the atom bomb essentially had the power of resolving the war itself which scientists like him failed to convey."

The use of the connector "No matter what" in the original sentence is irrelevant given the sense expressed in both the sentences it connects. Taking the context of paragraph into consideration, the use of the connector "Yet" complements the sense expressed in both the sentences.

3. B
Suggested changes for sentence 5, "For instance, the atom bomb was developed during the Second World War by the recommendations of the great Albert Einstein - who is accepted as the father of modern physics - in fear of the Germans developing it and using on the Allies."

The original sentence lacks a comma after the thought extension phrase "For instance". Also, the use of dash to link two or more ideas and make a point has been incomplete. Option B offers solutions to both of these errors while others do not.

4. C
The following sentence, if inserted before sentence 7, would best illustrate the main idea of the passage, "Nuclear fission that is used in the fuelling of the bomb, has the capacity to produce electrical energy which has turned out to be a major alternative later in the Twentieth Century."

The main idea of the passage is the misuse of science regarding the development of the atom bomb during the Second World War whereas it could effectively be used in meeting the energy demands of the countries involved in the war. This is expressed explicitly in the sentence offered in option C which is at the same time coherent with the seventh and eighth sentence between which it is being suggested to be placed. Other options either lack coherence or are less relevant.

5. A
Sentence 4 is a fragment. "Which I doubt belongs to any other person. "

This sentence is an extension of the sentence preceding it. It does not complete the thought when alone and is thus a sentence fragment.

6. D
Sentence 3 sentence is not consistent with the author's purpose. "For example, for an air stewardess position, girls have to be no more than 163 cm tall; whereas for jobs in foreign affairs, Chinese diplomats are required to match their foreign counterparts."

The passage talks about the people who want to increase their height by undergoing a surgery and points out the minimum height requirements for getting a job that they wish to work in. However, the expression "no more than 163 cm tall" is a statement about a maximum not a minimum. IN addition, the sentence refers to Chinese diplomats who must 'match' the height of their foreign counterparts, which could be taller, and hence require surgery, or could be shorter and not require surgery.

7. B
The following sentence, if inserted after sentence 7, would best illustrate the main idea of the passage, "This artificial way of gaining height is turning out to be a new trend among the new generation in height conscious China."

The paragraph discusses about the application of leg surgery among Chinese young people to increase their height. This is best reflected in the sentence suggested in option B which also contributes to the cohesion of the second paragraph as well as allowing a smooth transition between the second and third paragraph.

8. B
Suggested changes to sentence 8, "Even parents approve of the idea, being fully aware of all the complications and they are willing to finance such a sophisticated surgery."

The usage of vocabulary is wrong in this sentence. The word "complexity" is an adjective noun used to describe detailed aspects of a given subject which is less relevant in this case. The word "labyrinth" is also incorrect in this context. The correct counterpart for "complexity" in this case would be "complications" which takes into account the length of the surgery itself and the agony, sacrifice and the commitment associated with it, all in one. Also the word "sophisticated", as suggested in options B and C in the place of "labyrinth" is more appropriate as it hints about the details of the surgery. Option B offers both changes.

9. A
Sentence 4 is a fragment. "Which I doubt belongs to any other person. "

This sentence is an extension of the sentence preceding it. It does not complete the thought when alone and is thus a sentence fragment.

10. D
Sentence 9 is the least relevant to the main idea of the second paragraph. "He is panicked by street dogs and neighbors' cats and to avoid them, he crosses to the other side of the street every now and then."

The second paragraph mainly talks about Luke's odd behavior while in a moving in a crowd, but sentence 9 shifts the subject to his strategy when he encounters cats and dog in the streets.

11. C
Sentence 4 contains a redundant phrase. "Which I doubt any other person belongs to other than him."

In this sentence the second "other" is redundant. It can be omitted.

12. B
The following sentence, if inserted before sentence 1, would best illustrate the main idea of the passage. "But that does not bother him; rather he always seems to be happy in being able to utter those two words."

The passage starts with the speculation that Luke is probably the only person happy with his peculiar character and style of living. This is reflected in the sentence which is suggested to be added as the last sentence. Other options do not offer the same relevance and coherence.

Conclusion

CONGRATULATIONS! You have made it this far because you have applied yourself diligently to practicing for the exam and no doubt improved your potential score considerably! Getting into a good school is a huge step in a journey that might be challenging at times but will be many times more rewarding and fulfilling. That is why being prepared is so important.

Good Luck!

FREE Ebook Version

Download a FREE Ebook version of the publication!

Suitable for tablets, iPad, iPhone, or any smart phone.

Go to
http://tinyurl.com/max7212

Endnotes

Reading Comprehension passages where noted below are used under the Creative Commons Attribution-ShareAlike 3.0 License

http://en.wikipedia.org/wiki/Wikipedia:Text_of_Creative_Commons_Attribution-ShareAlike_3.0_Unported_License

[1] Infectious disease. In *Wikipedia*. Retrieved November 12, 2010 from http://en.wikipedia.org/wiki/Infectious_disease.
[2] Thunderstorm. In *Wikipedia*. Retrieved November 12, 2010 from en.wikipedia.org/wiki/Thunderstorm.
[3] Meteorology. In *Wikipedia*. Retrieved November 12, 2010 from en.wikipedia.org/wiki/Outline_of_meteorology.
[4] Cloud. In *Wikipedia*. Retrieved November 12, 2010 from http://en.wikipedia.org/wiki/Clouds.
[5] U.S. Navy Seal. In *Wikipedia*. Retrieved November 12, 2010 from en.wikipedia.org/wiki/United_States_Navy_SEALs.
[6] Respiratory System. In *Wikipedia*. Retrieved November 12, 2010 from en.wikipedia.org/wiki/Respiratory_system.
[7] Mythology. In *Wikipedia*. Retrieved November 12, 2010 from en.wikipedia.org/wiki/Mythology.
[8] Insect. In *Wikipedia*. Retrieved November 12, 2010 from en.wikipedia.org/wiki/Insect.
[9] Blood. In Wikipedia. Retrieved November 12, 2010 from http://en.wikipedia.org/wiki/Blood.

Made in the USA
Las Vegas, NV
14 August 2023